KT-413-838

What Management Is

JOAN MAGRETTA, M.B.A., PhD., is an award-winning contributor to the Harvard *Business Review*, where she was the strategy editor during the 1990s. Before that she was a partner at Bain & Company, a leading management consulting firm. She is a Senior Institute Associate of the Institute for Strategy and Competitiveness at Harvard Business School.

NAN STONE, PhD., spent fifteen years at the *Business Review*, the last five as its editor-in-chief. She was the first executive director of the Peter F. Drucker Archive. She is now a partner at the Bridgespan Group.

Both live in Cambridge, Massachusetts.

JOAN MAGRETTA

with the collaboration of Nan Stone

What Management Is

How it works and why it's everyone's business

P

PROFILE BOOKS

For Ann Roy Luehrman,
An extraordinary woman

This paperback edition published in Great Britain in 2003 by
PROFILE BOOKS LTD
58A Hatton Garden
London EC1N 8LX
www.profilebooks.co.uk

First published in Great Britain by HarperCollins Business 2002

3 5 7 9 10 8 6 4 2

Printed and bound in Great Britain by
Bookmarque Ltd, Croydon, Surrey

ISBN 1 86197 645 3

Contents

Acknowledgements

Like most books, this one owes many debts. The oldest was incurred when I got my first taste of managerial responsibility in the late 1970s. A tome several inches thick, titled *Management*, was making the rounds. I picked it up without much enthusiasm, like someone forced to eat her spinach. The author was Peter Drucker, and his book was a revelation. By the time I put it down, I saw the world—and management's role in it—very differently. Convinced this was work worth taking seriously, I quit my job and went to business school. Twenty years later, I continue to discover just how wise an observer Peter Drucker has been. His influence pervades this book.

I am grateful to other wonderful teachers as well. Readers familiar with the general management perspective of the Harvard Business School will recognize my debt to the School, its curriculum, and its massive case research effort. Most of what I know about linking strategy and execution was learned on the job, from colleagues and clients while I was a consulting partner at Bain & Company, a firm which deserves its premier reputation. Those who know the work of Michael Porter will recognize how much I owe to his truly seminal work on competition and strategy. As an editor at the *Harvard Business Review*, I had the privilege of working with Porter and with other leading writers whose thinking has influenced my own. Many of those debts are reflected in the Selected Reading section at the end of this book.

Above all, I want to acknowledge the debt this book and I owe to Nan Stone, former editor of the *Harvard Business Review*. During her fifteen years at *HBR*, she worked with a who's who of prominent thinkers—selecting and shaping the management literature that has influenced practice around the world. If Peter Drucker has been, without his knowing it, this book's godfather, Nan Stone has been its godmother. Initially, the idea for the book arose from a long series of conversation we had about the enormous impact management has on the quality of our lives. Management matters to everyone and not just to those who choose the field as a career. That said, we felt that much of the serious work in the field was too hard to read—especially for newcomers—and certainly hard to get excited about. We wanted to convey to everyone, and especially to those in their early and mid-career years, what makes management work that is challenging, worth caring about, and worth doing well. If this book has succeeded at that goal, it owes a great deal to Nan's dedication in guiding me through draft after draft. Her advice on both substance and style is palpable on every page.

Many colleagues and friends made time to make helpful suggestions about earlier drafts of this book. Three of them went far beyond the call of duty: Louise O'Brien, one of the smartest executives I know, has generously shared her insights about how strategy is translated into performance. Timothy Luehrman is an extraordinary teacher and practitioner whose advice extended well beyond his specialty in finance. Alice Howard has been a wonderful coach and sounding board on the practical issues of managing nonprofit organizations.

In addition, Nan and I would like to thank Jeff Bradach, Jim Collins, Clay Christensen, Paula Duffy, Peter Drucker, David Lawrence, Ellyn McColgan, Michael Porter, and David Pottruck for the comments and suggestions they offered at various points while this book was being written. Rafe Sagalyn has been the wise counselor one hopes for in an agent. At The Free Press, Bruce Nichols's judgment and support have made this a better book. Lastly, special thanks go to my husband, Bill Magretta. If every author had as discerning and sympathetic a reader in-house, the world of books would be enormously enriched.

Preface

A Roadmap Back to Business Basics

During the 1990s, I was the senior strategy editor of the *Harvard Business Review*. There I got to see, and debate, most of the so-called "cutting edge" management thinking of the day. Month in and month out, writers, publishers and publicists announced the discovery of "groundbreaking" new ideas. No question about it, it was the decade of buzz. And most of the buzz shared a theme that can be summed up in four of the most dangerous words in any language: "This time it's different."

Dealing with change is one of management's most difficult responsibilities. But dealing *effectively* with change requires a clear understanding of what does not change. To know what really is different, you must first know what stays the same and why. This is a book about enduring fundamentals, ideas that have stood the test of time.

Since this book was first conceived and written, much has changed in the world. The boom of the 1990s has given way to a painful period of retrenchment and uncertainty. During the boom, it appeared that business leaders could do no wrong. In the ensuing bust, with many former icons toppled by corporate scandals, it appeared instead that business leaders simply did not know wrong from right.

Entrepreneurs have also lost much of their luster. During the boom, we believed they walked on water. Now, after trillions of dollars of market capitalization have vanished into thin air, we better understand that people who try to walk on water, and those who invest in them, will get soaked.

The public mood has swung from excessive exuberance to equally excessive cynicism in the space of only two or three years. This book offers a more balanced view. It contains a dose of realism about what management is, and some idealism about what it can and should be. Above all, it is a book about why and how management matters.

By 1999, I was convinced that such a book would be useful. By then it was clear to me that the stock market wasn't the only bubble ripe for bursting. There was also a bubble in the market for management ideas. The sheer volume of material aimed at managers made it increasingly difficult to see the forest for the trees. I wanted to lay out, in one clear volume, the core ideas of the discipline of management. Since its publication, readers and critics alike have welcomed it as a roadmap back to business basics.

Why is such a roadmap needed? Financial markets are self-correcting, given enough time. Dislodging widely-held misconceptions is more complicated. The most colorful excesses tend to disappear quickly. It didn't take long for people to realize, for example, that you couldn't value an Internet business by the number of "eyeballs" who viewed a web site. Nor did many people continue to believe for very long that Free Agent Nation, a brilliant slogan of the era, was a practical prescription for the workforce of the twenty-first century. Such buzzwords last just long enough to destroy economic value and disrupt people's lives.

But other ideas linger and do more pervasive damage. Imperceptibly, almost without being noticed, a number of distortions have seeped into the very core of management thinking and practice. They color the way managers approach the decisions that drive success or failure. What are the right goals for an organization? How do you design a business, not only to create value for customers but to capture some of that value for its owners? How do you organize? How do you use numbers to keep score and to define success? What is the role of values in an organization?

These are not abstract or academic questions. They are issues managers wrestle with every day. In the following pages, I have articulated the principles of management that remain relevant for all organizations in all kinds of markets. In that sense, this book is timeless. Written at the height of one boom, its principles will carry readers all the way through the next one, even if it is a long time in coming.

Since the book's hardback publication, however, readers have stressed its timeliness, asking me to highlight the particular distortions that plague today's thinking. Here, then, are the major ideas I believe are due for a correction—ideas which are at the heart of this book:

1. Perhaps the leading buzzword of the 90's economic boom was *shareholder value*. It was the one goal managers claimed to be pursuing above all others. But many companies lost their way because they confused the measurement of shareholder value (i.e. today's stock price) with the actual creation of it. Shareholder value is a result, not a goal. Embracing the wrong goal has led many companies astray.

2. Because the term *business model* was used so often during the Internet boom to give legitimacy to bad business ideas, the concept itself has been somewhat discredited. In fact, every viable organization—whether it is a business, a government agency, or a nonprofit—requires a sound business model. This is a powerful idea, but only if it is used rigorously.

3. Business strategy is NOT dead, as many in the 1990s

proclaimed. It has not been made irrelevant by the heightened pace of change, or by the new realities of the global economy. But strategy is not primarily about reinvention and radical transformation. Nor is it about being the best or the biggest in an industry. Strategy is about being different.

4. The organizational fads of the 1990s—for example, outsourcing and acquisitions—are dangerous because when it comes to organization, one size does not fit all. Properly understood, organization must always be strategy and market -specific.

5. Excellent performance is impossible without measuring the right numbers. As the corporate scandals of recent years have made clear, too many executives came to believe that the primary purpose of the numbers was to make their organizations (and themselves) look good. It is dangerous to use numbers, which are in fact management's only window onto reality, as window dressing.

6. When it comes to performance metrics, one size does not fit all. Matching an organization's measures to its mission is one of management's most difficult and creative challenges. This is true for businesses and nonprofits alike.

7. Long-term performance is impossible without the right values. During the boom, it was easy to believe that individual talent alone drove success. But a host of prominent business failures—from Andersen to Enron—have shown that talent and energy, absent integrity and trust, can be terribly destructive. What, then, are the right values for an organization? Again, the answer is, "It depends." Matching a company's values to its mission is another of management's most important challenges.

Joan Magretta, Cambridge, MA
March, 2003

Introduction
The Universal Discipline

From the outside, business can look like "a seemingly mindless game of chance at which any donkey could win provided only that he be ruthless. But that is of course how any human activity looks to the outsider unless it can be shown to be purposeful, organized, systematic; that is unless it can be presented as the generalized knowledge of a discipline."

—Peter F. Drucker

What were the most important innovations of the past century? Antibiotics and vaccines that doubled, or even tripled, human life spans? Automobiles and airplanes that redefined our idea of distance? New agents of communication, like the telephone and the television, or the chips, computers, and networks that are propelling us into a new economy?

All of these innovations transformed our lives, yet none of them could have taken hold so rapidly or spread so widely without another. That innovation is the discipline of management, the accumulating body of thought and practice that makes organizations work. When we take stock of the productivity gains that drive our prosperity, technology gets all of the credit. In fact, management is doing a lot of the heavy lifting.

The human ability to *manage,* to organize purposefully, is as characteristic of the species—and probably as old—as the opposable thumb. But the discipline of management is new. Its roots can be traced to the mid-nineteenth century. Its coming of age as a discipline, however, is an unfolding event of our lifetime. During the past several decades, management has discovered its true genius— turning complexity and specialization into performance. Even free agents owe their freedom to management's ability to make their specialized contributions productive.

One sign of this coming of age is the explosion of yearly M.B.A. graduates. In the United States, the number grew from just five thousand in 1960 to roughly one hundred thousand by the year 2000. Over the same period, what began as a trickle of writing about management has turned into a flood. Despite this sea of words—or maybe because the volume is so overwhelming—most people are more confused than ever about what management is, and the popular conception has a lot of catching up to do with the advancing state of the discipline.

As editors of the *Harvard Business Review,* we had front-row seats at the floodgates. Our mission was to help a wide audience of practicing managers and professionals gain access to the ideas of specialists who normally spoke to a narrow circle of insiders. We asked every author who they wanted to reach and why that reader would be better off as a result. We listened for the punchline or, in our shorthand, the *so-what.* Now it's our turn to answer those questions.

Most management books are for managers only. This one is for everyone—for the simple reason that, today, all of us live in a world of management's making. Whether we realize it or not, every one of us stakes our well-being on the performance of management. If we want to make better choices about the organizations we join, support, invest in, or start, we must know concretely what management is, and when it is good or bad. If we want to make smarter choices about our own careers—how we can translate our talents into performance, what we do that causes us to succeed or fail—we need to apply the discipline of management to ourselves. If we want better communities and a better world for our children, we need a clear-headed understanding of how management performs in the nonprofit sector, and how the discipline can be properly applied to fields such as education and health care.

Wherever our needs exceed our resources, we need management. Wherever we work or volunteer, we need management. Doing well in today's world—and even doing good—requires that we all learn to think like managers, even if that's not what we're called.

Unlike most other professions—law or medicine or accounting, for example—you don't need a license to practice management. In fact, it's the only field we can think of where practice precedes formal training. The Harvard Business School, for example, has traditionally required students to work before they will be considered for admission to the M.B.A. program. What you get from the education, the theory goes, will depend in part on the experience you bring to it.

The same will be true of this book.

Newcomers to the field will find an inviting, jargon free introduction to the basics. This is a book about a set of powerful ideas, but it conveys those ideas concretely, through stories about real people and organizations. If you find, as we do, that those stories are interesting, the book will give you a richer appreciation of the breadth and the difficulty of management's work. Looked at from a distance, it's easy to think that management is only about economics and engineering but, up close, it's very much about people. Rightly understood, management is a liberal art, drawing freely from all the disciplines that help us make sense of ourselves and our world. That's ultimately why it is work worth doing—and so hard to do well.

Readers with more experience will find a different *so-what*. The book offers a concise synthesis of important ideas and practices— for example, value creation, business models, competitive strategy, the 80-20 rule, performance metrics, decision analysis. We believe that these, and the many other ideas that constitute the core of the discipline, are meant to be used. We present them in a way that will help readers apply them across a broad spectrum of managerial and professional work, in commercial organizations and nonprofits. For those who find the language of management to be more of a barrier than an aid to understanding, think of this book as everything you wanted to know about management but were afraid to ask.

Readers who bring the most sophistication to this book will get something different, a framework for stepping back and seeing the big picture, as well as a clear articulation of important, but often unwritten, rules. They may also gain some insight into their own organization's performance and their own practice as managers. They will find, we hope, that, although this is a book about the basics, the basics aren't always obvious.

A Discipline Often Misunderstood

The emergence of a discipline propels any field forward. Society has always had *managers,* using the word loosely, to refer to people in positions of institutional power, such as owners and overseers. In the same way, we've always had doctors. However, until medicine became a codified discipline that could be taught, practiced, and improved upon, we didn't expect much from them. Today, there are better doctors and worse ones—individual practitioners differ—but the discipline of medicine has raised the performance level of the average physician well beyond the most gifted of his predecessors a century ago. In the same way, the discipline of management has made possible a world in which organizations are so integral to the fabric of our lives that we take them for granted.

Despite this unprecedented success, management remains the least understood of the professions that shape modern life. For many, management is something to be tolerated. The cynical view is that we've inherited a society of organizations, therefore we need management to run them. That's getting the story backwards, mistaking cause and effect. It's because we've become so good at managing that we choose to create organizations to achieve a vast array of purposes that none of us could achieve acting alone.

Management's growing effectiveness has made organizations the vehicle of choice for carrying out much of the work of modern society. From art museums and advertising agencies to zipper manufacturers and zoos, the variety reflects the breadth of human purposes. Management makes organizations possible; good management makes them work well. Over the past century, the discipline of management has transformed the experience of work and multiplied its productivity.

Yet we rarely see management in this light. While the reputation of business continues to rise, the reputation of management continues to decline. Can you remember the last time you heard a talented young person say that he or she wanted to be a manager? An entrepreneur, yes. A consultant or investment banker or venture capitalist, yes. A manager, not likely.

Ironically, the world's most admired manager, GE's legendary CEO Jack Welch, is part of the problem. In the 1980s, at a time when GE needed to be picked up by the lapels and given a good shake, Welch consciously rejected the word *manager*. It carried too much bad baggage. It smacked of control and bureaucracy. Welch was on a crusade. His call for *leaders* struck a responsive chord. Around the same time, Peter Drucker, the world's most widely read writer on management, also backed away from the label, shifting instead to *executive*.

Welch, Drucker, and others were on to something. The name

change helped to clear the way for a new attitude, a new focus on performance, and what it takes to produce it in a modern economy. At the same time, however, it also created more confusion about what management is and contributed to its disrepute.

For most of us, the direct experience of being managed has not been the high point of our working lives. Bad bosses abound, and we tend to equate management with the bosses fate has dealt us, with the personalities and the politics that can loom so large in our lives. The more we are left to infer what management is from the behavior of the individual who is our boss, the less likely we are to grasp the underlying method. It's no surprise, then, that we don't immediately think of management as one of the transforming innovations of modern civilization.

Indeed, for many people, one of the most positive aspects of the new economy is its promise to do away with management and traditional organizations altogether. New-economy apostles proclaim that technology and virtual organizations will make managers—and management itself—disappear. Self-organizing work teams will take the place of managerial hierarchies. Leadership will be everyone's responsibility. More and more of us will work independently, as free agents, rather than as employees.

There is enough reality in this scenario to make it seductive. Essentially, however, it is not only wishful thinking, but the conception of management on which it is based is fundamentally flawed. Supervision may be disappearing, but management isn't primarily about supervising others. Hierarchical corporate structures may be flattening, but management isn't primarily about occupying a privileged rung in the chain of command. Management's real genius is turning complexity and specialization into performance. As the world economy becomes increasingly knowledge based and global, work will continue to grow more specialized and complex, not less. So, management will play a larger role in our lives, not a smaller one.

This, then, is a fundamental paradox at the heart of modern economies: The more highly educated and specialized we become, the more we need other people to perform. The Internet, which allows so many people to work as individual contributors and to think of themselves as free agents or independent professionals, underscores this interdependency but, ironically, also makes it less immediately apparent. We think we live in worlds of our own and can contribute as individuals, but this is only possible because some form of organization makes the specialized work we do productive.

Management's business is building organizations that work. Underneath all the theory and the tools, underneath all the specialized knowledge, lies a commitment to performance that has powerfully altered our economy and our lives. That, ultimately, is why management is everyone's business.

Organizations are changing dramatically, and they are taking new forms but, without organization of some sort, nothing would get done. As competition forces organizations to become more flexible and as technology enables organizations to work in new ways, they are less likely to provide structure and stability in people's lives. Once we looked to organizations to place us in the right jobs, to look after our careers, to structure our working lives. That has become a thing of the past. Whatever forms they take, today's organizations demand greater initiative and responsibility from individuals. In essence, they demand that we all think like managers. Much as we now take charge of our own health rather than leaving it entirely to the doctors, working in a knowledge economy requires us to take charge of our own performance.

No one would question the proposition that effective participation in twenty-first century life and work will require basic computer literacy. We contend it will require basic managerial literacy as well. This doesn't mean that there is a canon of great management literature everyone should read, nor does it mean that everyone needs an M.B.A. Management is a discipline open to all who are willing to work at it. Some of the most prominent and effective managers in the world are self-taught. In fact, much of the codified discipline has come from observing what works and what doesn't. (Conversely, an M.B.A. is no guarantee that a person will be a good manager.)

Managerial literacy means that we will all need to learn to think like managers, whether or not that is what we're called. It means we will all need a working grasp of the discipline of management.

Not Another Management Book!

In 1954, Peter Drucker published a book often hailed as the best introduction to management ever written. Before *The Practice of Management*, there were books on accounting, books on sales, books on labor relations—books on all the many individual functions of management. But Drucker's book was one of the first to see management as a discipline and a coherent whole.

As a young man, Drucker sampled a variety of jobs, but the one that stuck was journalism. Through a lifetime of writing, teaching, and consulting, he never lost his reporter's nose for a good story. As recovery from World War II was shifting the locus of power to large corporations, Drucker realized that making sense of the modern world would mean making sense of management—a task he initially undertook by engaging in a study of General Motors. What ensued for Drucker was a life's work of explaining management, not only to the general public, but to managers themselves.

In the decades that followed, the number of people studying and writing about management grew exponentially. Academics who once looked down their noses at management began to take it seriously. Consultants found that publishing their ideas was a valuable form of marketing. By the 1990s, most writers understood there was enormous value in *branding* an idea: establishing a connection between your name and a program that organizations might want to adopt. Reengineering was an idea that launched a thousand books.

In fact, the number of books and major articles has grown to over two thousand every year. Most of these focus on a single idea, one piece of the management puzzle seen in depth, but also in isolation and often out of context. Because readers rightly want ideas they can use, the literature is full of lessons learned and concrete to-do lists—the ten things you can do today to be an effective leader or a savvy negotiator.

What's wrong with this picture? Do the math. Multiply the ten things to do by the two thousand publications and, suddenly, the simple list of ten has turned into an overwhelming and bewildering twenty thousand things to do—and that's just this year's crop of reading. The busier we all get, the more seductive a short to-do list becomes. But which list of ten fits you and your situation? How will you know if you've chosen the right one? This is the problem of advice without context. With the field fragmented into so many small pieces, how will you put Humpty Dumpty together again?

That is the goal of this book—to present a coherent view of the whole, of the work known as *general management*. This is not a how-to book. Its purpose is to explain the underlying *why* of both the theory and practice of management. It was written to help a wide audience understand the fundamental principles of the discipline that makes modern organizations—and modern prosperity—possible. You will still be able to laugh at Dilbert—management is easier to describe than it is to practice, and there will always be more of us who get it wrong than who get it right. But you will also understand what management is capable of on a very good day. And on those bad days when things are going wrong, you will be far more likely to figure out what needs to be fixed.

We use the word *theory* with some trepidation. The work of

management, the messy business of getting organizations and people to perform, is not particle physics. If you're looking for abstract formulations, you've come to the wrong book. But without a theory of some sort it's hard to make sense of what's happening in the world around you. If you want to know whether you work for a well-managed organization—as opposed to whether you like your boss—you need a working theory of management. Similarly, if your job includes hiring other managers or deciding which ones to promote, you need a theory of what management is.

Good theory doesn't give you today's marching orders in the form of a to-do list. Instead, it helps you to make sense of things. It helps you to see patterns, to separate what matters from what doesn't, to ask the right questions. That's always valuable, but never more so than when things are changing, as they most decidedly are today. Old rules of thumb, or even radical new rules, may help you cope with a well-defined problem. However, few of the important problems that plague us arrive neatly labelled. True mastery of change comes from understanding *why* the world works as it does. The more things change, the more fundamental principles matter.

During the past two decades, both the discipline of management and the context in which it operates have changed at least as dramatically as they did in the era in which Drucker first studied the modern corporation. Power has shifted from Washington to Wall Street to Silicon Valley, and now seems to be shifting back to Wall Street. Those are metaphoric places, of course, icons for the shift from political power to economic power, and from statesmen and national bankers to innovators, entrepreneurs, and captains of finance. Journalists, true to their calling, have been following the story as it unfolds, creating new publications like *Fast Company* and *Wired*, or relocating the center of gravity at older magazines and media outlets. Even *The New Yorker* has added a regular management feature.

Sometimes, the journalist's lens shows us our culture with clarity and insight. Often, however, it's like looking into a fun-house mirror. Some elements, the role of money, for example, are exaggerated beyond all proportion—the fabulous wealth created and destroyed in a heartbeat, the drama of the big deal, the daily swings of the financial markets. The popular press also knows that good stories need colorful personalities, hence the prominence of celebrity CEOs, and the endless curiosity about the lifestyles of powerful men and women.

With a grateful nod to Peter Drucker, then, the purpose of this book is to present management as a discipline, and to see it whole. Through the successes and failures of real organizations, past and present, we will explore the core concepts of management in their natural setting—at work. Our mission is to see the forest for the trees, and to present what can be complex ideas simply, but not simplistically. We will provide a sense of how management thinking has evolved and how the big ideas relate to one another. We try throughout to present these concepts not as technical tools—many textbooks do that far better than we could hope to do here—but as ways of approaching the questions that define a manager's world. Increasingly, those are everyone's questions.

How This Book Is Organized

The book is divided into two parts. The first part, "Design," deals with the big picture. Together the first four chapters answer the overarching question: *Why do people work together and how?* We create organizations to accomplish ends none of us could achieve acting alone. The design concepts presented in part I provide a disciplined way of thinking about those ends and about viable alternatives for achieving them.

The story begins in chapter 1 with *value creation*, one of the most abused buzzwords in the management lexicon. Far from being a meaningless platitude, however, value creation is the animating principle of modern management and its chief responsibility. Value creation answers the *why* part of management's basic question; it goes to the heart of an organization's purpose, the mission it exists to accomplish. An organization's business model lays out how it will accomplish its purpose, the system of players it must depend on to create value. This is the subject of chapter 2. "Strategy," chapter 3, addresses how that system will differ from competing alternatives and, by so doing, create enough value to satisfy its owners and to be self-sustaining. Chapter 4 completes the answer to the question by placing the people who work together inside (or outside) the organization's boundaries, and establishing the rules of engagement that will best align all the players in the common pursuit.

Value creation and business models tend to get short shrift in most management books. That's not the case with strategy and organization. For management writers, this is the battleground on which many bloody ideological wars are fought: whether it's one school of strategy versus another, or the chicken-and-egg argument over whether strategy or organization comes first. For the increasingly specialized academics who study management, this lively debate can be a good thing. But like all wars, these too have their civilian casualties, people in organizations, who are trying to get on with their jobs amid the confusion of competing claims and theories.

Having helped some of the most influential thinkers of the past couple of decades figure out how to present their ideas to the world, we are acutely aware of the chief points of contention. Our own approach is best explained, perhaps, through a metaphor. Start digging and you will pass through many layers of the earth's surface, each one genuinely different from the others. At some point, however, you will hit bedrock—the common layer underneath it all, the solid foundation.

Part I is our attempt to hit bedrock, to define the conceptual core of management. Anyone with experience inside an organization of any size will immediately associate these core concepts with an annual event called *planning*. Most organizations have their own versions of this corporate ritual. It is often tied to other important management processes such as budget setting or leadership-team building. While rituals give shape and structure to our lives, they can also become a substitute for the meaning they were initially created to foster. This has been especially the case with planning, which—like many organizational rituals—has taken on a life of its own.

Part I, then, puts aside the rituals and processes to focus on the meaning. The real output of planning isn't meetings or strategy books. It's insight as to where an organization is headed and what it needs to do to get there. Properly used, the core concepts of management can and should lead to powerful, practical insights. Because these are the high concepts, however, the buzz surrounding them can be deafening. We hope part I offers a refreshing take on the fundamentals, free of sound and fury.

Translating plans into performance—*execution*—is the subject of part II. Strategy—and the organizational design it implies—is a living blueprint for superior performance. But a blueprint is nothing more than a design. Creating that design may require both rigorous analysis and flashes of insight but, getting from the drawing board to reality is not *just* execution. Execution may lack glamor, but it's very, very hard to do. What happens when Tiger Woods picks up a golf club, or Murray Perahia sits down at the piano, isn't *just* execution. We all know exactly what they're supposed to do. The actual doing is a lot harder than it looks.

Here, the doing is also a lot harder than it sounds. Words like *execution* and *implementation* make management sound like nothing more than following a recipe, or carrying out a set of orders. In fact, execution requires both discipline and judgment, on the part of everyone in the organization, not just the people who

occupy formal management positions. Managers may be nomi-
nally in charge, but they are rarely in control of anyone's performance but their own. So, if everyone is to perform in ways that
will contribute to the organization's success, everyone has to
understand what success is and what will be required to achieve it.
Making this joint performance possible is often the most challenging part of management.

To begin with, everyone in the organization must be focused
on a common reality, even though it may be far from obvious to
everyone what *reality* is. To accomplish this, management relies
heavily on numbers, and chapter 5 looks at how good managers
know which numbers to focus on and why basic numeracy is so
powerful. Equally important, management must make the organization's purpose concrete, so that everyone can pull in the same
direction and all their efforts will add up to success. Chapter 6
explains how good performance metrics do this and, thereby, make
an organization's *real* bottom line clear.

Chapter 7 looks at how management deals with another of its
imperatives: balancing short-term and long-term performance.
Managers must commit resources today, in the face of uncertainty,
to create the future. In other words, they must know how to invest
and how to innovate—activities about which management has a
great deal to say. Managers must also keep themselves and everyone else focused on the critical tasks at hand, making sure that
resources are deployed where they're needed, and that the organization is constantly moving forward. This is the subject of chapter
8. Last not least, managers must engage the energies and talents of
individuals who are just that, uniquely individual. Chapter 9 looks
at why values are such an important part of management's work
and how good managers use, rather than abuse, them.

In one way or another, each of these "musts" goes against the
grain. Each requires us to act in ways that don't just "come naturally" for most people, and that rarely happen by themselves in

organizations. Wherever an unnatural act is critical to performance, the practice of management has given rise to a discipline, a way of thinking and acting that managers learn from each other. Part II is about these disciplines, which have evolved over decades of practice to meet the universal and enduring performance challenges that every organization must confront. While most good M.B.A. or executive education programs at least touch on the body of theory that underlies the big design concepts presented in part I, these performance disciplines are more likely learned apprentice-style, on the job.

The Case Method: A Word About Examples

To the extent that general management can be taught in the classroom or through books, it is best done by looking at case studies. It's not just that stories are more entertaining, although that is certainly true. It's that cases come closest to capturing the multidimensional nature of the work, the need to understand concepts in a specific context.

That said, there is an occupational hazard peculiar to those who write about living organizations. Management is the art of performance. It is also, like the performing arts, done in real time without a net, enacted in a present that is constantly passing. It neither stands still, nor looks back. Use living organizations to illustrate ideas and, inevitably, those organizations will change. Tomorrow's hero is today's chump—and vice versa. When writers extract a lesson or a concept that may be valuable to others, some mistake it for a blanket endorsement of everything that organization has done, and will do, for all time. It doesn't work that way.

Nevertheless, examples are the only way to show that the principles apply as much to Henry Ford in 1910 as they will to whomever makes the cover of *Fortune* or *Business Week* in 2010. A few companies we describe are very new organizations that may no longer exist by the time you read this. However, most of the organizations we've chosen have sustained performance over one or more decades, and their successes reflect more than one or two seasons of good luck. Even so, while some will undoubtedly continue to outperform, others surely won't.

Nothing that eventually happens, however, is likely to change the enduring principles these organizations were chosen to illustrate. Business news focuses on who's in and who's out. This book is about ideas with a longer shelf life. Henry Ford achieved a kind of greatness—and then, in subsequent decades, he not only floundered, he performed (and behaved) spectacularly badly. Nevertheless what he did will still help anyone understand what strategy is, and the relationship between strategy and organization. Similarly, we talk about Dell's or eBay's business models not because we believe those models will enjoy a thousand-year reign, but because they'll help you understand and evaluate any business model. And, finally, we talk about a host of nonprofit organizations—from The Nature Conservancy to the Aravind Eye Hospital in India—to suggest how broadly the concepts of management apply.

Part I

Design: Why People Work Together and How

A group of people get together and exist as an institution that we call a company so they are able to accomplish something collectively that they could not accomplish separately—they make a contribution to society, a phrase which sounds trite but is fundamental.

—David Packard,
cofounder of
Hewlett-Packard

Chapter 1

Value Creation: From the Outside In

Price is what you pay. Value is what you get.

—Warren Buffett

Value creation is a term that crops up so often and in so many contexts that it is tempting to dismiss it as just another business buzzword. It is anything but. Value creation is the animating principle of modern management and its chief responsibility. The phrase captures an important shift in mindset from managing the resources that go into work (the *inputs*) to managing performance (the *outputs*, or results). And, more than that, it reflects a view of what performance is and how organizations perform.

At the same time, it's an odd term whose meaning is far from evident. Why talk about "creating value for shareholders," if what you're really saying is that you're giving investors a good return? Similarly why the tortured phrase "creating value for customers," if all you mean is that you're giving them a good deal? What's especially odd, given the down-to-earth pragmatism of most managers, is how abstract the phrase is. When we think about the work real organizations do, we're more likely to think about the concrete things they make, or the services they provide, than about an abstraction called value.

Yet, management's mission, first and foremost, is value creation. In this chapter, we'll look at what this means, how the language of value came into use as the practice of management evolved, and why its abstractness is, in fact, a virtue.

What Is Value?

OnTimeAuditor.com is a simple and representative new economy business. Although Michael Harris didn't start the company until 2000, its roots go back to the 1980s, when he was working as a software developer. Harris was frustrated. Despite the fact that he used shippers who guaranteed on-time delivery or your money back, his customers often complained to him about late shipments. Time and again, he would hear from angry customers waiting for their packages but the carriers themselves never said a word about the delays.

Out of frustration, Harris developed tracking software, which alerts the sender whenever a delivery arrives past its guaranteed delivery time. This software became the basis for OnTimeAuditor.com. Here's how the business works: OTA's customers pay a monthly fee of $9.95 to use Harris's software. It notifies them when shipments they have sent to their customers are late. Armed with this information, they can then demand a refund from the shipper, typically ten to twenty dollars per package. As of spring 2000, when the service started, the software worked for FedEx and UPS, and the company was planning to add other carriers over time.

What value does OnTimeAuditor.com create for its customers? That depends, in part, on how many packages they ship. According to industry estimates cited by the company's co-founder Robert Morse, roughly 5 percent of the 16 million packages FedEx and UPS ship each day arrive late. That's eight hundred thousand packages, give or take and, since the average shipping fee is about twelve dollars, all told, they represent more than $10 million a day in potential refunds. A company that ships, say, 100 packages a month, would collect roughly $1,000 a year in refunds. So, if the system really is easy to use, and it imposes no other costs on its customers (and both of those are critically important assumptions), the value to customers is pretty simple to follow. For roughly $120 a year, our imagined customer can "buy" concrete and measurable savings of $1,000. For that customer, the service would create $880 of value in a year.

In industrial markets—or what is now often called *B2B* (business to business)—calculating the economic value of a good or service (that is, determining how much it's worth) is often fairly straightforward. The value created for the customer usually resides in time or labor or materials saved, and those savings can be quickly translated into a cash equivalent. Like most business-to-business vendors, OnTimeAuditor.com bases its sell directly on the dollar value its service creates. It even gives its customers an on-line calculator, so that they can track their savings.

But the service may also create value in another way. Recall Michael Harris's motivation for creating his software in the first place. If you are notified that a shipment you sent a customer is late, you can at least do something about it. So, for some clients, OnTimeAuditor.com may be creating far more value in the form of better customer relationships. The fact that it's harder to quantify doesn't make it any less real.

In consumer businesses, which account for two-thirds of the U.S. economy, there is usually a difficult-to-quantify leap to be made between the product or service delivered and the value created. Charles Revson, the cosmetics executive, once quipped that his industry sells "hope in a jar." For consumers, value often resides in such intangibles: in a product's look and feel (the colorful iMac, for example, or a design by Armani); in emotions such as nostalgia; in status and prestige. When people are asked what single item they'd rescue in the event of a fire, they seldom talk about the most expensive thing in the house. They talk about the family photographs. Even here, where value seems to defy definition, it is possible to tease out its chief components.

Before George Eastman put picture taking within everyone's reach in the 1880s, it was strictly the province of professionals. The process was messy and cumbersome. Liquid chemicals had to be poured onto glass plates, then subjects had to sit motionless for what seemed like an eternity, because those wet plates needed long exposure to light.

Eastman figured out how to make photography easy. He embedded all the chemistry on to lightweight paper film; and then designed a camera so simple anyone could use it. But, at twenty-five dollars, three months' wages in 1888, the Kodak was beyond the means of most people. So, Eastman went back to the drawing board. The result, twelve years later, was the Brownie, a device so uncomplicated and easy to manufacture that Eastman could sell it for one dollar. Finally, he had achieved all the components of value for a mass audience—ease of use, affordability, family photos that people treasured. Eastman the entrepreneur became Eastman the industrialist. The company he founded, Kodak, has prospered for over a century.

Customers Define Value

Value, then, not only takes many forms, it comes from many sources—from a product's usefulness, its quality, the *image* associated with it (by advertising and promotion), its availability (how easy it is to get, where it's sold or distributed), the service that accompanies it. The more intangible the value appears, the more important it is to recognize that value is defined by customers, one person at a time. Many people love fast food, but many hate it. Some people swear by their cell phones, others swear at people who use them in public places. A two-week vacation in a primitive nature sanctuary is one person's heaven, and another's hell.

Even in our simple industrial example, in which value is easily quantifiable, the value created by OnTimeAuditor.com will differ from customer to customer. The same service would create vastly more value for a customer who sends ten thousand packages per month than it would for one who sends only a hundred. Or, it would create more value for a business whose customers are particularly sensitive to timely and reliable deliveries. The point, which is both subtle and obvious, is that value is defined not by what an organization does but by the customers who buy its goods and services.

When management defines its objective as creating value for customers—as opposed to selling software or manufacturing film—the language serves to remind us of this basic principle. The term also reminds us that organizations are means to ends, not ends in themselves. They exist to serve the needs of people who are outside them. This is what differentiates an organization (of whatever kind) from a tribe, a social club, a family, or any other group that focuses only on the well-being of its members. One of management's chief responsibilities is to remember this external orientation and to remind others about it constantly.

Constant reminders are necessary, because it's natural for people who live inside an organization to get wrapped up in what they do, to focus on what they make, and the craft, whatever it might be, that goes into the making. It's natural, in other words, to focus on what economists term *inputs*, all of the many elements that constitute a job well done. One of the most powerful insights of modern management, however, is that there is really only one test of a job well done—a customer who is willing to pay for it.

Customers don't care how much hard work or ingenuity goes into designing a product. Nor are they always properly impressed by genuine breakthroughs, as every new generation of entrepreneurs is destined to discover. In the late 1990s, for example, Silicon Graphics had some of the best engineers in the Valley. The company poured millions of dollars into the development of interactive television, which its engineers rightly thought was a groundbreaking technology. But ITV turned out to be a product in search of a customer. Kittu Kolliri, one of the lead engineers, explained the company's colossal flop this way: "We got all wrapped up in the technology. We all thought, 'Dammit this technology is so cool. It must bring value to someone.'" It didn't. Bringing value to some vaguely defined someone isn't good enough. Only real customers write real checks. Only by meeting the needs of customers, as customers themselves define those needs, can an organization perform.

Value as Efficiency: The Manufacturing Mindset

These days, there is so much talk about customer focus that it's easy to think that this perspective is axiomatic, that no one could conceive of a business working any other way. In fact, the insight that customers, not producers, determine what constitutes value is relatively recent. Historically businesses were defined by what they made. A company was in the steel business, say, or the coffee business or the car business. The way to succeed was to figure out how to make more steel or coffee or cars using the same or fewer resources.

The challenge, in other words, was to increase productivity, and the way to do that was to make the production process as efficient as possible. This focus on efficiency made great sense in an industrial economy in which demand far outstripped supply. Management's mission was making more things, more cheaply. When George Eastman introduced the Kodak camera at twenty-five dollars in 1888, he sold only 13,000. When he introduced the simpler, cheaper one-dollar Brownie in 1900, Eastman sold 150,000 cameras in the first year alone. Making the product affordable created a vast new market.

The prophet of efficiency was Frederick Winslow Taylor.

Born in 1856 to a prosperous Pennsylvania family, Taylor could have gone to Harvard, but chose manual work instead. After an apprenticeship as a pattern maker and machinist, he signed on as a common laborer at Midvale Steel, one of the industry's leading companies. Within six years, Taylor rose through virtually every position in the plant to become its chief engineer.

Taylor approached the task of efficiency with the discipline of a scientist—observing, measuring, and recording even the most apparently obvious tasks. In 1898, he was hired as a consultant by Bethlehem Steel at the prompting of Joseph Wharton, one of the company's owners and the founder of America's first business school at the University of Pennsylvania. At the company, Taylor undertook many of the experiments described in *The Principles of Scientific Management* (1911). Taylor's message was clear: However simple a task may seem, you need to study it systematically to determine the "one best way" to do it.

When Taylor walked through Bethlehem Steel 100 years ago, he saw an army of 600 men wielding shovels, each one doing pretty much what came naturally. The men used the same shovel to move ore, at thirty pounds per load, and rice coal, at less than four pounds. For Taylor, the science of shoveling lay in determining the load at which a "first-rate man" (that is, a man both willing and able to shovel) could do the greatest day's work. After careful experiments, Taylor got his answer: twenty-one pounds. As a result, the company began to provide specialized shovels for the men, each tailored to its task: "a small shovel for ore, say, or a large one for ashes."

Taylor claimed that, as a result of changes like these, productivity soared, and the company's costs dropped—even after allowing for increased wages for the men. These were the parameters of value in Taylor's world, and they were all contained within the walls of the factory. Scientific management, with its emphasis on measurement and analysis, was the first true management discipline. At its heart is a basic tenet: Never assume that the best way to do something is the way it has always been done. In other words, never take the work for granted.

Neither Taylor nor scientific management has a very good reputation these days, although the widespread pursuit of best practice is a direct legacy of his work. Taylor was tarred by the labor politics of his era, while Taylorism became synonymous with the deskilling and dehumanization of work. Nonetheless, developed economies owe much of their prosperity to Taylor and his followers. Throughout the twentieth century, we have caricatured efficiency experts and cursed the pursuit of efficiency, all the while reveling in the wealth that greater efficiency has produced. Taylorism (like modernity) may be a Faustian bargain, but it is hard to imagine what our lives would be without it.

The real limitation in Taylor's approach was its singleminded focus on manufacturing efficiency. He assumed that value meant making whatever you were making more efficiently. Taylor wasn't wrong, he was just narrow in how he thought about management's mission. It didn't occur to him to question whether you were making the right things to begin with, or whether you could create more value by undertaking broader missions.

Taylor's was a reasonable assumption to make at the beginning of the twentieth century, when the number of goods produced was relatively small, and the major challenge was simply to produce more of them at lower cost. But by the middle of the twentieth century, scarcity was giving way to consumer plenty, especially in the United States. The question—what is value?—needed a new answer.

The Marketing Mindset: What Does the Customer Value?

When Vienna-born Peter Drucker decided, in 1943, to spend two years studying General Motors from the inside, he put his career at risk. Back then, it was not academically respectable to study something as mundane as a profit-making corporation. Today, when even Oxford University has a business school, this statement seems implausible. However, at the end of World War II, the corporation was *terra incognita* and the work of its managers largely unexplored.

In his landmark book, *The Practice of Management,* he offered a critical redefinition of value. Efficiency was necessary, but not sufficient. Customers don't buy products, Drucker observed, they buy the satisfaction of particular needs. This means that what the customer values and buys is often different from what the producer thinks he sells.

Defining value as efficiency, as Taylor did, led to an intense focus *inward,* on what the company makes and how it makes it. This has become known as the *manufacturing mindset.* It suggests that you start with what you make, you price it based on what it cost you and then you sell it to the customer. It is a make-and-sell model of how a business works.

Drucker urged a completely new way of thinking. If you want to understand value, don't focus inward on what you make, the way the engineers developing ITV did. Look through the customer's eyes, from the outside in. The new perspective advocated by Drucker and others became known as the *marketing mindset.* It is a sense-and-respond model that starts with what the customer wants, and with how much she or he is willing to pay for it. This determines both what you make and how much you can spend making it. This shift in perspective was absolutely fundamental, the managerial equivalent of discovering that the world wasn't flat after all.

It quickly led to a crucial distinction between *selling*—convincing a customer to buy whatever it is you make, and *marketing*—understanding what customers value so that you can work to satisfy their needs. To help managers develop this outside-in perspective, Drucker formulated a series of deceptively simple questions: "What is our business?" "Who is the customer?" "What does the customer value?" These questions, which have been repeated like a catechism by managers around the globe, disciplined managers to look at the work of any organization through the eyes of its customers.

Today, these are questions that must be asked by everyone who works, and not just by managers. They are especially powerful questions for people who do knowledge work, for the analysts or systems engineers or logistics experts whose work isn't visible in any product. The analogous questions are: "Who depends on my work?" "How do they use it?" and "Why is it valuable to them?" Lacking direct contact with external customers, you can identify your internal customer(s) and ask them pointedly how you could become more valuable to them.

The same thinking applies to independent professionals as well. Lawyers and consultants, for example, have historically fallen into their own version of the manufacturing mindset, defining their product as "hours of advice," "relationships," or "studies." But is this really what their clients value? A management consulting firm, Bain & Co., was started by a handful of individuals who thought hard about these questions and came up with this answer: our clients want better business results, not reports. They're not buying hours of advice, they're buying greater profitability—profits at a discount.

Entrepreneurs who succeed always create value for customers, although initially they may do so more by instinct and accident than by conscious design. But over time, organizations (especially large ones) tend to take on lives of their own, and can lose touch with the market surprisingly quickly. This is why Drucker's discipline remains such an important antidote to the natural tendency to focus inward, on what you make and do.

Moreover, answering these apparently simple and obvious questions turns out, in practice, to be neither simple nor obvious. Almost every organization probably has at least a few different ways to define its business. If McDonald's had defined itself as being in the hamburger business, for example, it might have concentrated all of its attention on making the world's best hamburger. The result might well have been a better-tasting and more expensive hamburger, but it certainly wouldn't have been a quick, affordable meal. Managers who properly define their business can systematically focus on delivering what their customers truly value—in this case, speedy service. Had the company thought of itself as being in the hamburger business, we might never have heard of McDonald's at all.

Who the customer is isn't always immediately obvious either. The longer version of George Eastman's story has some important twists and turns. He ended up creating one of the broadest-based mass-consumer businesses of all time. But that's not the customer Eastman set out to serve.

Eastman's first company manufactured dry plates—glass plates precoated with emulsions. This innovation meant professional photographers no longer had to mix and pour their own chemicals. It made their lives easier and somewhat more mobile, but the glass plates were still heavy items to lug around. As the dry plate business grew more competitive in the 1880s, Eastman worked feverishly on an entirely new solution. He wanted to replace the heavy glass plates with film made out of lightweight paper, coated with an emulsion, then mounted on a roll holder. By 1885, Eastman was ready to bring his great innovation to market.

It was a colossal failure. Convenient, yes, but there was a trade-off. The image quality wasn't up to professional standards. When photographers rejected Eastman's innovation, he came close to losing his company. Then came the insight about value that changed history. Maybe Eastman had the right product but the wrong customer. If professional photographers didn't value the kind of pictures his film produced, ordinary people would love them. If only he could make a camera so simple that anyone could use it.

What could be simpler than a black box with one button for the shutter and a winding key to roll the film? When you finished your 100 snapshots, you sent the whole camera to Rochester, and it came back to you reloaded and ready to go again—along with your finished prints. Creating value for ordinary people forced Eastman to develop not just a manufacturing business (making cameras and film). He needed an accompanying service business (turning negatives into prints) as well. Kodak's motto and marketing slogan: "You push the button. We do the rest."

George Eastman turned a small dry-plate business into one of the largest and most successful consumer businesses of all time. And he did it by thinking about who the customer is and what the customer values.

Maximizing Shareholder Value: The New Mantra

In the prosperity that followed World War II, marketing was management's rising star. *Efficiency*—doing things right—remained important. However, now *effectiveness*—doing the right things, that is, the things that customers valued—became even more important to performance. At least, that was the theory. In practice, marketing often turned out to be just selling in disguise. The new corporate marketers were masters of "hidden persuasion." Advertising was criticized as a cynical game of manipulation, designed to convince people to purchase things they didn't need.

There was a growing sense in the late 1960s and 1970s that management was becoming more insulated and more arrogant— more interested in its own power than in delivering value either to its customers on Main Street or its owners on Wall Street. The emergence of lean and aggressive Asian competitors in the 1970s and early 80s brought the question to a head. America's premier industry—the auto industry—was losing ground rapidly to Toyota, Datsun, and Honda, companies whose names had been virtually unknown less than a half-dozen years before. Detroit had lost touch with its customers, continuing to produce big gas guzzlers when people wanted small, fuel-efficient cars.

But it was Japan's manufacturing prowess that unleashed the real value revolution. Japan's success in autos continued well after the gasoline lines of the 1970s were a distant memory. Compared to Detroit's product, Japan's cars were solid, reliable, and built to last. Customers were won over by the simple fact that Japanese cars gave them both higher quality and lower cost at the same time. In other words, they offered better value. And customers were quick to vote with their wallets.

The auto industry was just one of several to be shaken to its core. Almost overnight, or so it seemed, Japan had gobbled up 20 percent of the American steel market. Across the entire manufacturing sector, millions of factory jobs were eliminated, leaving behind a vast Rust Belt, a term that evoked the Great Depression and the devastation of the Dust Bowl.

Management had taken much of the credit for America's prosperity in the 1950s and 60s, and it had certainly rewarded itself handsomely for that success, with soaring compensation packages, and such perks as corporate jets. If management took credit for years of smooth sailing, where was it while the ship was going down? Why were executives doing so well when their companies were performing so poorly?

Those questions were posed by a new breed of shareholders and financial operators, the corporate raiders and leveraged buyout experts. They charged that management was too focused on the bureaucracies it had created, that it wasn't doing its job of faithfully representing the interests of the corporation's owners. Instead, too much of the pie was wasted on managerial empire-building at the expense of profits for the company's shareholders. Jack Welch later described the seismic shift in characteristically blunt terms: "The complacent and timid had a date with the hostile-takeover people."

The 1980s witnessed an unprecedented war—often referred to as *the battle for corporate control*—between owners and management. In the press, this battle was often portrayed as a raid by unprincipled sharks snapping up innocent victims, breaking them into pieces and selling them off for a quick buck. But if you stop to think about it, the only reason the pieces could have been worth more than the whole was if the whole were poorly designed or badly managed. The hostile-takeover people Welch referred to figured out how to unlock the value trapped in underperforming companies, and use it to wrest control of the companies from CEOs like Nabisco's Ross Johnson, whose fleet of twenty-six jets was known as Ross's Air Force. In the end, shareholder value emerged not only as the mantra of the decade (and beyond), but as a guiding principle of management and a law of survival: Maximize value for shareholders or you will be ousted by the unrelenting discipline of the capital markets.

The upshot was that managers became dramatically more responsive to the interests of owners, and more aware of the direct link between delivering value to customers and creating value for shareholders. In some industries, satisfactory underperformance had been a kind of gentlemen's agreement. Those days were gone. Now, shareholders would set the bar, and the capital markets would define performance. The ensuing pressure for higher returns sparked furious debates about corporate purpose, which still flare up from time to time. Economists like Milton Friedman argue that the shareholder must always come first, that the goal of management, purely and simply, is to maximize shareholder value. Others—especially in Europe—argue that management has broader obligations to society as a whole, to provide employment and stability for communities.

Although individual managers may differ in their social philosophies, no contemporary CEO can afford to take the capital markets for granted or ignore their discipline. Before the 1980s, a company that created enough value to cover its costs could safely, and sometimes comfortably, underperform relative to its potential. Value creation was sufficient. Since the 1980s, any public corporation that doesn't maximize value risks losing control to a new owner. This is what people mean when they talk about the *discipline* of the capital markets. The new discipline has changed the practice of management forever. And while nonprofits and family-owned businesses remain somewhat insulated from this pressure to perform, they feel the ripple effects of this change as well. Thus, it has become more critical than ever for executives to understand the process of value creation and the drivers of superior performance.

How Is Value Created?

In the 1980s and 1990s, as pressure from all sides—competitors, customers, and shareholders—continued to escalate, managers were compelled to re-examine everything they did. One consequence was growing interest in an economic concept introduced into management thinking in Michael Porter's *Competitive Strategy* (1980), a landmark book that almost singlehandedly created the new field of business strategy. This concept is the *value chain,* the sequence of activities and information flows that a company and its suppliers must perform to design, produce, market, deliver, and support its products.

The managerial consequences of value-chain thinking are enormous. The first consequence is that you begin to see each activity not just as a *cost,* but as a step that has to add some increment of value to the finished product. Over time, this perspective has revolutionized the way many organizations define their business. Twenty-five years ago, for example, if you wanted to trade stocks, you had to pay hefty commissions to a broker. Behind that broker was a fully integrated set of activities that ranged all the way from doing research and analysis of securities to executing your trades to sending you a monthly statement. The costs of all those activities were buried in the price of the commission.

Charles Schwab created the company that bears his name—and a new category known as *discount brokerage*—around a different value chain. Not all customers want advice, so why should they have to pay for it? Take away all the activities needed to give advice, focus instead on executing trades, and you can create a different kind of value: low-cost trades that make stock ownership accessible to a wider customer base. Matching the *value chain*—what's inside the company—to the customer's definition of value was a new way of thinking just twenty years ago. Today, it has become conventional wisdom.

A second major consequence of value-chain thinking is that it forces you to see the entire economic process as a whole, regardless of who performs each activity. If you want to build a fast-food business around consistent, perfect French fries, as McDonald's did, you can't make excuses to a customer because the potato farmer you buy from lacks proper storage facilities. The customer doesn't care who's at fault. The customer cares only about the quality of his fries. So, McDonald's has to make sure that, one way or another, all the potato growers from whom it buys can meet its standards.

The implications of this interdependence are profound. Managing across boundaries, whether these are between the company and its customers, or the company and its suppliers or business partners, can be as important as managing within one's own company.

The year 2000 was full of news about automobile tires. The big headline was the massive recall by Firestone. Instead of celebrating its hundredth anniversary, the company was preoccupied with a public-relations nightmare. Tire failures were linked to dozens of deaths and hundreds of accidents. Firestone was buried in a massive recall of millions of tires, a deluge of bad press, and a growing number of lawsuits.

Firestone was not the only company suffering, however. This was also a nightmare for Ford, because most of the faulty tires were sitting on Ford Explorers. The fact that Ford didn't manufacture the tires was essentially irrelevant to the angry customer who owned an Explorer. Firestone was an important link in Ford's value chain and, in the summer of 2000, Firestone destroyed value for Ford's customers and its shareholders.

A story grabbing less attention was also about tires. In this case, it was a business-as-usual story, not a crisis. Toyota saw a new approach to tire making at a small Japanese company, and it began lobbying the big tire makers to get with the program. The headline in the *Wall Street Journal* captures the message: TOYOTA URGES TIRE COMPANIES TO ADOPT NEW DESIGN TO REDUCE COSTS AND WEIGHT. Why should Toyota care? Because it knows that its customers want cars that will cost less and be more fuel efficient. If this means that Toyota must push its suppliers into a new technology that will allow Toyota to create more value for car buyers, then that's what Toyota will do. In fact, Toyota's success as an automaker has largely been due to its ability to manage its suppliers.

Over the past two decades, management has been transformed by these insights about how value is created and the need, therefore, to manage across the organization's boundaries. For example, a decade ago, purchasing was a low-profile function, the goal of which was to get the best terms for a predetermined set of items. Today purchasing has evolved into *supply-chain management*, and this is a real shift, not just an instance of title inflation. Supply-chain management reflects a far more systematic way of thinking about how a company creates value for its customers: through what it buys and not just the price it pays, through gains in speed and flexibility as well as cost, through access to a supplier's know-how and innovative capability as well as its goods.

The value revolution we've been describing has worked its

way into every aspect of a company's business. When organizations look from the outside in, they often see a brave new world of innovative offerings in the form of solutions and value-added services aimed at meeting customers' needs, not simply selling them products. To get a sense of how dramatically this can transform a company, consider how GE has changed under Jack Welch's leadership. Once one of the world's premier industrial companies, GE now gets 80 percent of its profits from services.

GE's locomotive business, one of its oldest, illustrates the shift. GE's engineers have been building locomotives, the workhorses of the industrial economy, since 1895. And until recently, says Welch, "building the latest high-efficiency this and high-efficiency that was the route to epaulets on your shoulder." That was the manufacturing mindset. When GE looked at the business through the customer's eyes, however, it realized that what the railroads want isn't bigger and more powerful locomotives. It's the ability to ship the most freight at the least cost, which means that what they really need is a locomotive in productive service more of the time. In other words, they need a way to schedule locomotives better, fix them faster when they break, and so on. Solve those problems, and you will improve the performance of the railroad, which is, after all, what the customer really wants.

For GE's locomotive business the shift in mindset from inputs to results, from product to solution, was like flipping a light switch. Once the light went on, GE came up with a whole slew of services such as computer-aided dispatching systems to help railroads manage their fleets more efficiently. Thanks to equipment placed on the locomotives, the railroads can track the location of any train at any time, and so can GE. When a train breaks down, no one has to call the company for advice. GE can go directly to the site and get it back in service.

As manufactured products have become increasingly commoditylike, and therefore less valuable to customers, GE has not been alone in discovering that often more money can be made from the services related to a product than from the product itself. Consider the service contract that you are offered when you buy a new television or computer, or the financing available from the dealer who sells or leases you a new car. Much of IBM's success in the 1990s reflected its shift in strategy from hardware to solutions.

The same logic is being applied in the most mundane consumer businesses as well. Martha Stewart's web site sells all kinds of household goods at premium prices. A brand-name iron selling on the site for $125, for example, is sold elsewhere for ninety dollars. Asked about the difference, a company spokesman explained that by "providing things like instructions" they are "adding value to the customer." Click on the iron and you'll learn how to iron a shirt. Are customers paying for this advice, for the convenience of ordering from the web, or for the seal of approval the Stewart brand may connote? It could be any, or all, of the above. In the new economy, value lies increasingly in such intangibles.

The Right Discipline for Nonprofits: Mission, Not Markets

Today, there are more than one million nonprofit organizations in the United States. Together, they make up over 10 percent of the economy. They are estimated to control nearly $2 trillion of assets. The sector is important not just because of its size, however, but because we depend on it to do so much of the work that is vital to our well-being as a society.

Our stake in how nonprofits perform, as individual organizations, and collectively as a sector, is enormous. We rely on them for education and health care. They promote the arts and protect the environment. We count on them to minister to people in need. Yet, for many experienced executives and volunteers in the sector, the old joke that managing a nonprofit is like herding cats accurately sums up the state of play.

Why are nonprofit organizations so notoriously difficult to

manage? In a sense, for-profit managers have it easy. The economic value they exist to create is far easier to define and measure than social welfare. Consider the value created by Habitat for Humanity International, the organization which has helped construct housing for more than one-half million people around the world since it was founded in 1976. Habitat's mission is to eliminate poverty housing by helping poor people build simple, decent, affordable houses. The houses are built by volunteers, working side by side with the prospective homeowners, under the supervision of a skilled professional. Local merchants donate building supplies. Done this way, with most of the actual construction work occuring on Saturdays, each project takes several months. Clearly, this is not the most efficient way to build houses.

But the houses aren't the whole story about the value Habitat for Humanity creates. Its mission isn't simply to be an economically efficient home builder. If that were the case, it would probably raise money and buy professionally built houses instead. An important part of Habitat's mission is partnership. The value it creates goes beyond the houses, to the social capital that's generated when individuals contribute to their communities and to the welfare of others.

This is as important to Habitat's mission as the houses it builds. As one staff member explains, "The ultimate goal is not the house but the people who participate in the building of that house, the families who will live in that house, the society that they are a part of, and [the volunteers] participating in so many ways." Habitat's many constituents—its volunteers, its donors, its home recipients—will be indicators of performance. If any of them cease to believe that the organization is creating value, they will go elsewhere. But those signals aren't as strong as the market forces that discipline businesses to maximize the value they create. Well-run nonprofits have to take on the more difficult challenge of imposing mission discipline on themselves.

They must ask their own set of deceptively simple questions. "What is our mission?" "What is the unique value we exist to create?" "Who will support us in fulfilling our mission, and how can we align their interests with our mission?" Mission, not "customers," must be in the driver's seat. "Customers" can lead mission-driven organizations astray. Consider New York City's Bronx Zoo and its panda policy.

Nothing draws crowds to the zoo more than the lovable panda bear, but New York's Bronx Zoo, one of the finest in the world, doesn't have any pandas. Does this mean it's not doing a good job of creating value? The answer depends on the value the zoo exists to create, and that, in turn, depends on its mission.

In 1895, the New York Zoological Society (NYZS) was established to create a zoological park, advance the study of zoology, protect wildlife, and educate the public. If we define the zoo's customers as the providers of financial support, then the City of New York has been an important customer. In the 1980s, when Ed Koch was New York's mayor, the flamboyant politician felt that getting pandas for the zoo was key to his popularity. He spent years lobbying Beijing for a pair of the appealing creatures. When his efforts succeeded, the zoo was obliged to accept them.

What happened next led to a rethinking of panda policy in scientific and government circles. The species now numbers only about one thousand bears; increasing the total is tricky because females ovulate only once a year. When the female in the pair Ed Koch brought to New York ovulated, nothing happened because the male wasn't yet of breeding age. An opportunity critical to the survival of the species was lost.

In 1993, the Bronx Zoo's parent changed its name to the Wildlife Conservation Society. The name change was a useful reminder of the organization's mission—and of the primacy of conservation above all. Its purpose, its mission, is to marshal public support and scientific expertise to save threatened species. The panda is one of those threatened species. The society's leaders have to weigh a difficult tradeoff. Displaying pandas in zoos is one very effective way to generate public support. Some people argue that this is a crucial aspect of conservation because we only protect what we care about. But as long as the society's scientists believe that housing pandas in American zoos does the species more harm than good, the Bronx Zoo will remain panda-less. The only thing that will keep management on track when it faces tough choices like these is the organization's mission.

Nonprofits are hard to manage because they lack the unambiguous feedback loop a paying customer provides a for-profit organization. With most nonprofits, there is a disconnect between the people who fund the organization and its beneficiaries. While thinking of important constituents as *customers* can be helpful—especially in making notoriously bureaucratic organizations more responsive to the people they exist to serve—it can be misleading as well.

Consider the American Red Cross, which accounts for over half the nation's blood supply. Who is the Red Cross's customer? Is it the hospital that uses the blood, or the donor who rolls up his sleeve? Until the 1980s, the question wasn't very important. Like all nonprofits that rely on the generosity of donors, the Red Cross could treat all of its important constituents—its beneficiaries, its funders, its volunteers—as if they were customers. Attention and resources could be spent making the process of giving blood so attractive that donors would cheerfully participate in the annual blood drive. It was a community-spirited event that made everyone feel good.

The world has changed. Since the 1980s, the HIV epidemic has made blood safety a top priority, and more intrusive screening of blood donors a necessity. Donors with risk factors must be turned away. At the same time, hospitals are under intense pressure to contain costs, and blood is a major item on their budgets. This has forced the Red Cross to become more cost conscious, cutting back, for example, on smaller, poorly attended blood drives. Not all donors have been happy about these changes.

One thing is clear. To carry out its mission in this new environment, the Red Cross has had to make the proper and critical distinction between a customer and a donor. As a result, it has had to make some difficult changes. It has had to think about its donors more as a supply-chain manager would think about its suppliers. In this instance, the equivalent of market forces made these changes inevitable. Regulatory agencies dictated strict standards for blood management and hospitals began behaving more like real customers, exerting pressure on costs. In other words, the Red Cross was forced to define value from the outside-in.

Most mission-driven organizations don't face such strong external forces, although, in general, donors are demanding greater accountability, and government funding is increasingly performance-based. Where market discipline is lacking, however, management must substitute mission discipline as its own form of outside-in thinking.

Value Is a System

We began this chapter with the assertion that management's chief responsibility is to create value. But whether it has delivered on its responsibility isn't management's call to make. That is the province of outsiders who are free to decide, day by day and year after year, whether they will continue to support that organization.

Determining who the relevant outsiders are may be management's single most critical decision. As we've seen, this determination is usually a lot easier to make in the for-profit sector than it is in the nonprofit sector. But even in the business world, customers aren't the only constituency modern management has to satisfy. In reality, every successful organization depends on multiple players, each of whom defines value in a particular way.

Shareholders and others who provide investment capital define value in financial terms that are easy to measure. For employees, the equation is more complex. They value today's wages and health benefits, but they are also likely to prize such things as training or stock options whose value lies in the future. Value for employees may also reside in such noneconomic factors as job satisfaction, status, or pride. Suppliers may value long-term relationships and the chance to develop cutting-edge technology as much as they care about price alone.

Modern management's challenge is to ensure that each of these necessary players will choose to participate in the system that creates value for all of them. The term *value creation* captures this larger, more systemic understanding of performance in a way that earlier definitions of performance did not. Value creation includes the industrial era's focus on efficiency, as well as the consumer era's focus on the customer, on quality, and on choice, but it is capacious enough to include all of modern management's other constituents as well. That is why we said earlier that the term is usefully abstract.

In the next chapter, we'll explore how business models help you understand and manage the system that creates value. We'll see how a business model works as a system for converting insight into enterprise.

Chapter 2

Business Models: Converting Insight to Enterprise

"Business model" is one of those terms of art that were central to the Internet boom; it glorified all manner of half-baked plans. All it really meant was how you planned to make money. The "business model" for Microsoft, for instance, was to sell software for 120 bucks a pop that cost fifty cents to manufacture. The "business model" for Healtheon was to add a few pennies to every bill or order or request that emanated from a doctor's office. The "business model" for Netscape was a work in progress; no one really ever did figure out how to make money from Netscape; in its brief life Netscape had lost money. The "business model" of most Internet companies was to attract huge crowds of people to a Web site, and then sell others the chance to advertise products to the crowds. It was still not clear that the model made sense.

—Michael Lewis,
The New New Thing

Like value creation, the term "business model" has become a buzzword of the Internet economy, a term that has lost some of its meaning through sloppy usage. Like "value creation," it is a useful and important concept. This chapter will explain what a business model is and how you can tell a good model from a bad one. Although the term may be new, the idea is timeless. Every organization—be it new economy or old, for profit or not—needs a viable business model.

Let's start with a definition. A *business model* is a set of assumptions about how an organization will perform by creating value for all the players on whom it depends, not just its customers. In essence, a business model is a theory that's continually being tested in the marketplace. When EuroDisney opened its Paris theme park in 1992, it assumed that the enterprise would work in pretty much the same way that Disney's American theme parks operated. Europeans, Disney thought, would spend roughly the same amount of time and money per visit as did Americans, on food, rides, and souvenir shopping.

Each of these assumptions turned out to be wrong. For example, Europeans didn't graze all day long at the park's various restaurants as Americans did. Instead, they expected to be seated at precisely the same lunch or dinner hour, which overloaded the facilities, and created long lines of frustrated patrons. As a result of these miscalculations, EuroDisney was something of a disaster in its early years. It became a success only after a dozen or so of the key elements in its business model were changed one by one.

The discipline of management operates from a theory of the business, from a model of how the whole system will work. Major decisions and initiatives all become tests of this model. Profits are important not only for their own sake, but also because they tell you whether your model is working. If you fail to achieve the results you expected you re-examine your model, as EuroDisney did. It is the managerial equivalent of the scientific method, starting with hypotheses, which are then tested in action, and revised when necessary.

It's probably no accident that the term itself came into use with the rising popularity of the spreadsheet. What once had been a laborious task—laying out the future revenue and cost projections of an enterprise in order to create a business plan—suddenly became easy. More than that, constructing a spreadsheet forces you to specify the relationship of each of the pieces of a business to the whole. Once you've created a spreadsheet, you can ask what-if questions—what if the market grows by 25 percent a year, for example—and with a few easy keystrokes you can see how any change plays out on every aspect of the whole. In other words, you can model the behavior of a business.

Before this was possible, business historians like Alfred Chandler and Peter Drucker described the whole in words. The field known as *general management* aimed to explain through case studies, or mini-histories, how all the pieces and policies of corporations like Sears and General Motors fit into a coherent whole, creating value for shareholders by delivering value to customers. Case studies reveal an important insight. Underpinning every successful organization—whether the people who run that organization know it or not—is a business model that any sensible person can understand after the fact. We want to emphasize this point because, in the annals of business history, few of the creators of great business models actually set out, with analytic forethought, to develop anything as abstract as a model.

Why, then, has the term become so hot in recent years? In large part, the answer lies in the explosive growth of new ventures sparked by the Internet, which made it technically possible to conceive of new theories for how an enterprise might work. Historically, entrepreneurs persuaded other people to invest in their fledgling businesses by demonstrating success. In other words, they had to make a profit before anyone but family and friends would give them money. For a short time in the late 1990s, the old rules for funding new enterprises were temporarily suspended. Entrepreneurs persuaded people to invest in earlier (and earlier) stages. Since there couldn't be any profits yet, the company's business model was invoked to give some legitimacy to what remained an unproven idea. The business model became a kind of shorthand for "Trust us. We know what we're doing. Someday we'll make money."

A good business model, however, does a lot more than legitimize entrepreneurs in search of capital, and it captures much more than how an enterprise might make money. Business models reflect the systems thinking that is so central to management.

A Good Model Tells a Good Story

Model is one of those loaded words that conjures up images of white boards filled with arcane mathematical formulas. Business models are anything but arcane, however. A business model is a story of how an enterprise works. Like all good stories, a business model relies on the basics of character, motivation, and plot. For a business, the plot revolves around how it will make money. For a social enterprise, the plot is how it will change the world (or at least, its targeted corner of the world). In both cases, the characters must be precisely delineated, their motivations must be plausible, and the plot must turn on an insight about value.

Here's an example of one of the most successful business models of all time, one that's 100 years old, but still widely imitated to this day. Like many great business models, it began with a very human experience of frustration, and not with the analytic efforts of a planning committee. It developed as much through serendipity, experimentation and luck as from any great foresight. It's the story of American Express and the accidental creation of travelers' checks.

American Express started out as a regional freight express business in 1850. In 1892, its president, J. C. Fargo, took a European vacation and had a hard time translating his letters of credit into cash. "The moment I got off the beaten path," he said on his return, "they were no more use than so much wet wrapping paper. If the president of American Express has that sort of trouble, just think what ordinary travelers face. Something has got to be done about it." What American Express did was to invent the travelers' check and, in the process, one of the most valuable business models of the past 100 years. What's the story this business model tells? Who are the key players and why is each of them motivated to play his part?

For customers, the story is straightforward. In exchange for a very small fee, travelers could buy both peace of mind (the checks were insured against loss and theft) and convenience (they were also very widely accepted). Until the advent of credit cards, in fact, the checks were almost the only solution to the problem of getting money while traveling, especially abroad.

Merchants were also key players in this tale. They accepted the checks because they could trust the American Express name, which was like a universal letter of credit, and because, by accepting them, they attracted more customers. The more other merchants accepted the checks, the stronger any individual merchant's motivation became not to be left out of the game.

As for American Express, it had discovered a riskless business, because customers always paid cash up front for checks that would be accepted wherever and whenever they chose to use them. Therein lies the special twist to the plot, the underlying economic logic that neither Fargo nor American Express had anticipated, but which turned what would have been an unremarkable business into a money machine.

The twist in the plot is something called *float*. In the normal course of almost every business known to man, companies have to pay out all the costs that go into a product (the labor, the raw materials) before they can sell it and recover their costs. They have to tie up capital, often borrowed money, and they have to keep their fingers crossed that they will be able to sell their product at a good price when they do bring it to market—allowing them to repay their loans and make a profit as well.

American Express Travelers Cheques turned the normal business cycle of debt and risk on its head. Since people paid for the checks before (and often long before) they used them, American Express was getting something banks had long enjoyed—the equivalent of an interest-free loan from its customers. That's float. Moreover, some of the checks were never cashed at all, so Amex made money on the float, and then some more money on the unused certificates. A brilliant business model was born by one chance event (the trip) compounded by another (the discovery of float).

The fact that Fargo didn't know how this story would play out when he set it in motion is irrelevant. After the fact, the story is clear and compelling: We see who the characters are, why they will behave as they do, and the underlying economic logic that drives the plot and makes a self-sustaining system of the whole. Now that the story is known, others can adapt its principles to a variety of businesses. Gift certificates, for example, are widely used by retailers not only to increase their sales, but also to take advantage of float.

What Makes a Good Story a Better Story?

We said earlier that behind every successful organization is a relatively simple business model that everyone can understand. We'll go a step further. Behind every successful organization is a business model that in its time was revolutionary. In our enthusiasm for e-commerce business models, it's easy to lose sight of the simple fact that new business models are at least as old as the pin factory, with its revolutionary use of specialized labor, that Adam Smith described in *The Wealth of Nations* (1776). In its day, the business model underlying General Motors, for example, was as breathtakingly new and exciting as the one eBay is built on.

By definition, a successful business model represents a better way than the existing alternatives. It may be better for a discrete group of customers, or it may completely replace the old way of doing things—and, thus, become the standard for the next generation of entrepreneurs to beat. Nobody today would head off on vacation armed with a suitcase full of letters of credit. The travelers check was a quantum leap advance over that existing technology. Fargo's business model grew out of an insight about an unmet need. His new product changed the rules of the game, in this case, the economics of travel. The costs that traveler's checks eliminated (like the fear of being robbed or the hours spent trying to get cash in a strange city) weren't strictly monetary, but that didn't make them any less real. The checks removed a significant barrier to travel and enabled many more people to take many more trips.

Creating a new business model is not unlike writing a new story. At some level, all new stories are variations on old ones, reworkings of the universal themes that underlie human experience. Similarly, new business models are all variations on the universal value chain that underlies all businesses. Broadly speaking, this chain has two parts. Part one includes all the activities associated with making something: design, the purchase of raw materials, the manufacturing or service-delivery process. Part two includes all the activities associated with selling something: finding and reaching customers, transacting a sale, distributing the product or delivering the service. As in a good novel, the particulars of every business model will be unique but, in one way or another, every business model is a story about the basic human activities of making and selling. The plot may turn on designing a new product for an unmet need, as it did with the traveler's check. Or it can turn on a process innovation, a better way of making or selling or distributing an already-proven product or service. The twist in a new business model is almost always a variation on some aspect of an existing value chain.

In the course of this chapter, we'll look at several business-model stories. Each began with an entrepreneur who thought he saw a new and better way to do something than the way it was then being done. Each offers a unique take on the age-old problems of making and selling—and each tells us something about what makes a good business model.

Michael Bronner and Eastern Exclusives

Michael Bronner is one of the pioneers in what has come to be called *relationship marketing*. The firm he founded, Bronner Slosberg Humphrey, now part of Digitas, was among the country's first and most successful direct marketing firms. BSH harnessed the power of information technology to help its clients gather better data about their own customers and then use it to create more targeted and effective marketing programs. Relationship marketing represented a new solution to a universal problem: how to reach customers.

The seeds for this sophisticated new-economy company were sown in 1980, when Michael Bronner was a junior at Boston University. Like his classmates, he had occasionally bought books of discount coupons to be used at local stores and restaurants. Students paid a nominal fee for the coupon books, effectively allowing them to buy discounts at a discount. The more Bronner thought about the process, though, the less sense it made. Yes, the books created value for the students, but they had the potential to create much more value for the merchants who stood to gain by increasing their sales of pizza and haircuts. Unlocking that potential was the problem Bronner set out to solve. The key, he realized, was wider distribution, putting a coupon book in every student's backpack.

How could Bronner do that? First, Bronner had to think like a student, which wasn't too hard, since he was a student. He understood that students were often strapped for cash. What would happen if he gave the books away for free? How could they refuse something for nothing?

Second, Bronner had to solve the problem of physical distribution. His solution was clever. He went to the dean of the university's housing department and made a proposal: He would assemble the coupon books and the housing department could distribute them free to every dorm on campus. This would make the department look good in the eyes of the students, who were a notoriously tough crowd to please. The dean agreed.

Now, Bronner could make an even more interesting proposal to neighborhood business owners. In exchange for a small fee to appear in the new book, the merchant's coupon would be seen by all 14,000 residents of BU's dorms. Bronner's idea took off. Before long, he had extended the concept to other campuses, then to downtown office buildings. Eastern Exclusives, his first company, was born.

Bronner's innovation wasn't the coupon book, but the distribution system he designed and the business model he created around the simple insight that the merchants, not the students, were the coupon's real customers. It was the merchants who had the strongest motivation to pay for Bronner's service. The more coupons Bronner could get into students' hands, the more he could increase the merchants' sales, so the more they would be willing to pay. That's the revenue side of the model, the story of how Bronner got paid.

The model was equally ingenious on the cost side. Think of all the activities and resources it takes to run a coupon business, the making and selling components of its value chain in other words. Someone has to make the rounds to sign up the merchants. Then there is the cost of printing the books. Finally, and most important, there is the cost of distributing the books, of actually getting them into the users' hands. Coopting the university housing office into doing the distribution not only raised the value to the merchants (because it enabled them to reach more students) but also lowered Bronner's distribution costs to zero. In sum, the model has all the elements of a good story: a cast of characters with credible motives, a problem to be solved by an insight about value, and a first-rate plot with an economic twist that increases revenues and lowers costs.

Bronner's coupons were a cost-effective marketing tool for small businesses seeking new customers. They were a low-tech solution for helping local merchants grow within local markets.

Pierre Omidyar and eBay

At the other end of the spectrum—in terms of scale, scope, and technical sophistication—is eBay, the first and, to date, the most successful person-to-person trading community on the Internet. Bronner's business model offered an efficient way for dozens of small merchants to reach thousands of new customers. eBay raises the ante by orders of magnitude, harnessing the power of the Internet to bring millions of buyers and sellers together electronically.

Like so many innovative enterprises, eBay got its start because someone saw a better way to do something. In this case, the entrepreneur was Pierre Omidyar, who describes himself as an "anticommercial" former software developer. Omidyar's girlfriend collected Pez dispensers, and she wished there were a way to trade with other collectors over the Internet. To make that possible, he designed a small on-line trading post, Auction Web, which launched in 1995, well before the Internet had entered most people's consciousness.

As word of the site spread, more and more collectors began to list a wide variety of goods. Initially, postings were free, but soon Omidyar began to charge a small fee (twenty-five cents per item) to defray the cost of maintaining the site. In 1996, his pet project became a full-time job and, a year later, it was a a flourishing venture-backed business. Omidyar knew he needed a CEO with brand-building experience and, early in 1998, he recruited Meg Whitman for the job.

Whitman saw immediately that eBay had the ingredients to make a successful business model. First, as she recalls, unlike many early Internet ventures, "This was actually the creation of something that *couldn't be done* offline. I thought that was highly compelling. The second thing that struck me was the emotional connection between eBay users and the site." Whitman joined Omidyar in March of 1998; they took the company public six months later. At the end of its first day of trading, eBay had a market value of almost $2 billion. By the summer of 2000, eBay accounted for 90 percent of the on-line auction business with 15 million registered users. One year later, that number had doubled.

How does eBay's business model work? In essence, the company runs a never-ending yard sale with the entertainment value of an auction. Unlike its real-world analogues, however, eBay's virtual marketplace is huge—and hugely efficient. That size, made possible by the Internet, is the key to this story.

You don't have to be an economist to understand why size is essential to create an efficient market that gives buyers access to the goods they want to buy and sellers access to customers who will offer them the best price. Anyone who has ever held their own yard sale or tried to dispose of a less-than-precious family heirloom or bought a house will understand the problem. Within any pool of buyers, some are willing to pay more than others. In economists' terms, the item gives those buyers greater *utility* (value) and their *willingness to pay* is, therefore, higher. If a market is large enough to be efficient, there will be enough buyers competing against each other to drive the price up to the level of the buyer for whom the item has the greatest utility.

Pulling together a large enough pool of buyers costs money, however. Tack up a sign in front of your house announcing your yard sale and it will be a very local affair indeed, limited to the handful of potential customers who happen to pass by at the right time. Put an ad in the local paper, and you can attract a few more buyers, but you pay a price to do so. The bigger the audience you try to reach, the more it will cost you. Ultimately, you will bump up against the constraint of distance. People will come only so far to see your old rocking chair.

As the seller in such a scenario, your power to impose what you consider to be the right price is limited, since your alternatives usually aren't very attractive. If your rocker doesn't sell, you can put it back in the attic or you can toss it onto the junk heap. It may be a real bargain, but only if the right buyer happens to find it. With too few buyers and too few goods to attract more, the yard sale is about as inefficient a market as you could hope to find. Some people may find it a pleasant way to pass the time, but it's no way to make a living.

A variety of retail business models are variations that attempt to fix the economics of this flawed story. The secondhand dealer attempts to turn the yard sale into a viable business by putting himself in the middle: buying up used goods (at yard-sale prices), then adding value by using his market knowledge to select goods customers will want, and offering a greater variety of items under one roof. But the dealer also incurs added costs: he spends time acquiring the goods, he pays rent, and he may get stuck with owning inventory that no one will want to buy. The dealer, then, is banking on customers' willingness to pay a premium price that will compensate for these added costs. The consignment shop is a variant on this model that allows the dealer to avoid the inventory risks, since he pays the owner of the goods only after the item is sold.

eBay solves the problem of inefficient local markets by bringing millions of people together in cyberspace. The more buyers eBay can attract, the more sellers, and vice versa. This is what's called the *network effect,* and therein lies the economic twist to eBay's story. Size explains not only why buyers and sellers are drawn to eBay, but how eBay works as a business. eBay gets a small fee for every listing (ranging from twenty-five cents to two dollars), a larger fee (ranging from $2 to $49.95) for added services, such as highlighting the listing, and a potentially larger fee (ranging from 1.25 percent to 5 percent of the sale price) when a transaction takes place. In other words, eBay makes money in a variety of ways: from the absolute number of listings and transactions, by providing extra marketing services to sellers, and by encouraging items to sell at higher prices.

That's the revenue side of the story, and eBay's model encourages buyers and sellers to behave in ways that support each of those revenue sources. Since size matters, eBay's basic listing fee is low so that it won't deter anyone from playing the game. eBay's auction format is not only entertaining for buyers, but it may also result in higher selling prices, as buyers step in at the closing minutes, sparking bidding frenzies.

What about the cost side of eBay's business model? The story begins, of course, with the Internet's dramatic lowering of the cost of reaching and connecting large numbers of people. eBay's business model couldn't work without it, but it is just part of the story. When an auction ends, if there's a winning bid, eBay notifies both seller and buyer by e-mail, and leaves it to them to work out the logistics of payment and shipping. The company never takes possession of the goods or carries any inventory. It incurs no transportation costs. It bears no credit risk. And it has none of the overhead that would come with those activities.

The burden of enforcing honest trading and good behavior is likewise largely a community affair. For example, buyers are encouraged to submit feedback after every sale; this feedback is then added to the users' profiles, which are posted on the site. Participants with good marks get color-coded stars, while those who receive too many negative comments are dropped. The community ethic has always been important and, from its inception, eBay knew that weakness here could bring the company down, so its managers have also invested in trust-enhancing services such as escrow accounts.

For sellers, eBay is a wonderfully inexpensive marketing channel, providing easy, low-cost access to a large pool of buyers. In fact, despite eBay's popular image as a national yard sale, the lion's share of its business no longer fits that description. eBay has become the marketing and distribution arm for thousands of small-business people. They provide the merchandise and eBay— for a small transaction fee—supplies the customers. This is the underlying economic logic that drives eBay's business model. eBay lowers the cost of reaching customers for thousands of small businesses, giving them the kind of scale economies that formerly only large companies could enjoy. With eBay in the story as an intermediary, thousands of small businesses became viable for the first time.

As this pattern of sellers has emerged, new companies have sprung up to serve them by providing the related services (like shipping and billing) that running a business requires. These third-party companies complement eBay, making it even more attractive to small businesses. In fact, it's fair to say that eBay has as many (if not more) entrepreneurs to its credit as all the venture-capital firms combined. As one satisfied user said, "eBay is capitalism for the rest of us."

Organizations are always works in progress. This may be where our analogy between business models and story telling breaks down. No business model can be fixed forever on the page. The story keeps going, it evolves, it changes. In the first five years of its life, eBay was a phenomenal success because it was one of the first companies to develop a viable business model for the Internet, one based on providing a service for which people were willing to pay, and not on advertising. In fact, early on, the rejection of on-site advertising was an essential piece of eBay's story, because its founders felt that advertising would compromise the sense of community that was fueling its growth.

That may always be true—or eBay's view may change as the enterprise evolves. Doubtless eBay will continue to test this and other elements of its model, and doubtless eBay will change. Like all organizations, *how* it will change depends in large part on market power, and on the peculiar blend of psychology and economics that underlies market behavior. In the next section we'll explain what that means.

How Markets Work

After an organization has been spectacularly successful or unsuccessful, it's not hard to derive its business model and see what makes it work—or the flawed assumptions that led it to fail. Before the fact, the picture is filled with all sorts of uncertainties. Uncertainty doesn't mean that there's no basis for making reasonable assumptions, however. Much of what ultimately determines a business model's success is the behavior of people and organizations in markets

For example, Michael Bronner understood how the likely behavior of the students, the local merchants, and the university officials would determine both his pricing and his costs. Each one got something of value at a good price. His insight about what each of them would value allowed him to put together a new system—a lower-cost solution to the merchants' marketing problem—by introducing a new character, Bronner, the marketing agent. Similarly, eBay has been insightful about the psychology and the economics that draw collectors, bargain hunters, community seekers, and small-business people to its site. eBay's model works because every essential player, pursuing his own self-interest, gets something of value.

Like these, every successful business model presents clearly drawn characters whose behavior is at least plausible, if not inevitable. Models that fail often do so because they are premised on fuzzy characters or unlikely behavior. Consider the rapid rise and fall of Priceline Webhouse Club, Inc. This was an offshoot of Priceline.com, the company that introduced the concept of name-your-own pricing to the purchase of airline tickets. Wall Street's early enthusiasm encouraged CEO Jay Walker to extend his concept to groceries and gasoline.

Here's the story Walker tried to tell. Via the web, millions of consumers would tell him how much they wanted to pay for, say, a jar of peanut butter. Consumers could specify the price, but not the brand. So, if they bid on peanut butter they might end up with Jif or they might end up with Skippy. Webhouse would then aggregate all the bids and go to companies like P&G and Best-foods and try to make a deal. Take a dollar off the price of the peanut butter, and we'll order a million jars this week.

The idea behind Webhouse was that it would aggregate customer demand and thereby serve as a power broker for individual consumers. By representing millions of customers who each needed to buy peanut butter—or diapers or gas—the company would be able to negotiate discounts with the giant consumer companies and gasoline dealers and then pass on the savings to its customers, taking a fee in the process.

What's wrong with this story? It assumes that companies like P&G, Kimberly Clark, and Exxon will want to play this game. Think about that for a minute. Big consumer companies have spent decades and billions of dollars convincing us that their brand is better. Their very lifeblood is brand loyalty. (This is why coupons are consumer companies' preferred way to discount.) The Webhouse model teaches consumers to buy on price, brand be damned! So, would the manufacturers want to help Webhouse undermine both their prices and the brand identities they'd worked so hard to build? The story would require a key player to act out of character—and against its own rational self-interest.

Market Relationships Are Power Relationships

Embedded in every business model is a set of hypotheses about how the world works. Although it starts with who customers are and how you think they will behave, it also includes all the rest of the players on which the model depends. Overall, the model explains why and how the organization will be able to pull together the talent, capital, and suppliers it needs. No organization can exist very long without each of these resources, albeit in different combinations and to different degrees. Thinking managerially means looking at these resources through the lens of markets: seeing the world as a set of discrete markets for talent, capital, and supplies.

As consumers, the markets with which we're most familiar are product markets. We tend to focus on them one product at a time and to be most concerned with issues of choice (can I get what I want?) and fairness (am I happy with the price I have to pay?). Moreover, we tend to see price mostly as an expression of value (is this car or computer worth what it costs?). When managers look at the markets in which they must participate they see something else. They see a web of power relationships that sets limits on their organization's ability to perform. The configuration of this web is a constraint that ultimately determines both a company's costs and its prices.

For a business, survival demands that prices be set somewhere between what it costs to make the product and its value to the customer. If the price is lower, the company goes broke. If it's higher, there won't be any customers. Market structure usually tells managers whether they will have the power to price their product in the survival zone and where in that zone they will be: whether they will enjoy the fat margins of drug companies, for example, or the razor thin margins of supermarkets. (*Margins* are the spread between the cost of a good or service and its price.)

A company's costs are determined by the markets in which it is a buyer looking for the best price. It buys the raw materials and components it needs in supplier markets. It "buys" the employees it needs via a labor market. It buys funds to fuel its business (to pay its suppliers, say, or to build facilities) through the capital markets. In each instance, the prevailing market price (prices for products and raw materials, wages for employees, interest rates for capital) reflects the balance of power between the buyer and the seller.

At one level, this power relationship is simply a matter of supply and demand. The price of software engineers and web-site designers, for example, has soared in recent years, because the demand for their skills far exceeded the supply. Hiring companies had few alternatives, and so bid ever-higher prices for people who could fill the jobs. Sellers of talent have been in the driver's seat, and the result has been what's called a *seller's market*.

At another level, however, the power relationship also reflects a phenomenon known as *industry structure*, one important aspect of which is the relative concentration of buyers and sellers in an industry. Consider the U.S. auto industry, where the Big 3 (Ford, GM, and DaimlerChrysler) purchase components and subassemblies from thousands of suppliers. Or discount retailing, which is similarly dominated by three big players, Wal*Mart, Kmart, and Target. When just a few major companies buy from lots of suppliers, the buyers are likely to dominate the market. For the most part, unless the item being supplied is highly proprietary or scarce, the buyer will call the shots—and dictate a price that won't allow much in the way of profits for the seller.

What gives large buyers so much power? Because each seller supplies just a small percentage of the buyer's needs, he can credibly threaten to take his business elsewhere. For the seller, however, this would be a disaster, because each of these big buyers accounts for a large percentage of its sales. The seller, then, is more dependent on the buyer than the buyer is on the seller.

The balance of power is reversed when a few suppliers serve a fragmented market of buyers or the seller is bigger relative to the buyers' needs. Consider the market for the little plastic hangers that retailers use to display garments in their stores. Not long ago, there were many suppliers serving the Big 3 discounters. A company like Kmart could use its purchasing power of $40 million a year to negotiate a good price (good, that is, for Kmart).

Then, Tyco International, a diversified corporation with a penchant for building market power through acquisitions, came along and consolidated the supply side. One by one, Tyco bought up all the companies that sell plastic hangers to Kmart. In less than four years, Tyco amassed 70 percent to 80 percent of the plastic garment hanger market, amounting to roughly $400 million in sales in 2000 (or ten times the size of Kmart's purchases). Now, the shoe was on the other foot, and Tyco could raise the price of hangers—to the point, according to the *Wall Street Journal*, that customers were crying foul and complaining that Tyco was abusing its market power. When suppliers are concentrated, customers—especially in the short term—may have nowhere else to turn. Tyco has figured out how to trump the power of even the biggest retailers.

Like Tyco, both Priceline.com and eBay set out to change the balance of power by altering the structure of existing markets. eBay's success and Priceline's failure illustrate the enduring fundamentals of market power, even in the Internet age, and they call to mind a very old story indeed, the riddle of the chicken and the egg. eBay grew by creating a service customers were willing to pay for. Over time, as the company attracted some 30 million users and became the distribution channel on which so many sellers depend, the balance of power has shifted decisively toward eBay, a fact that will surely weigh in its future decisions about its business practices such as advertising.

Webhouse chose to take a different path. Like many Internet-based businesses, it took on a set of dominant, established players. Its business model cast Webhouse as a power broker. But to be a power broker, it needed a huge base of loyal customers. To get that base of customers it first needed to deliver discounts. Since the consumer companies refused to play, Webhouse had to pay for those discounts out of its own pocket. A few hundred million dollars later, in October 2000, it ran out of cash—and out of investors who still believed the story.

Dell: Eliminating the Middleman

One of the best business-model stories of the past two decades has been that of the Dell Computer Corporation. Michael Dell captured the attention of the business press as one of the proto-typical entrepreneurs of the age—the young computer whiz who drops out of college and makes a fortune creating his own technology company. But Michael Dell's really powerful insights haven't been technological ones. They've been business insights. Back in the early 1980s, he looked at the personal computer business and saw a better way, a way that would take a lot of unnecessary cost out of the system and make it possible for people to buy what they wanted at a lower price.

The better way was selling direct to customers, bypassing the dealer channel through which personal computers were then sold. Instead, Dell would take an order from a customer and then buy and assemble the components he needed. That meant he didn't need plants and equipment to build the components, nor did he have to invest in research and development (R&D). The customer got exactly the configuration he wanted, and Dell avoided the reseller's markup.

It was a wonderful business idea. Dell could share the pool of money saved by eliminating the middleman with his customers: they got the technology they wanted at a lower price, and he made more profit than other PC makers. The "simple" story of Dell's direct business model is that it took an existing value chain and cut one unnecessary and costly step out of the process. (In economic terms, this is called *disintermediation*.) From the customer's perspective, this new value chain represented better value.

Eliminating the middleman turned out to have a host of other advantages that Dell didn't anticipate when he dropped out of college to devote himself full time to his company. Here is where we find the really interesting twist in the plot. By making products to order, Dell avoided all the costs and risks associated with carrying large inventories of finished goods. This would always have been a good thing, whatever the business environment. But in the economy of the 1990s, with its torrid pace of innovation, Dell's business model turned out to be a spectacular thing.

A mantra of the new economy, one that is recited somewhat automatically, is that value is shifting from things to ideas, from products to services. The success of Dell's business model demonstrates the extent to which even products are behaving more and more like services. What does this mean and why does it matter?

Inventory has always been the critical issue for a service business. If you're in the airline business, for example, you've got a lot of cost tied up in every flight. There's the cost of the plane and the fuel and the crew, and all these are fixed costs, because they don't change whether the plane is carrying three hundred paying passengers or thirty. To make money, you must fill the plane. You manage what the industry calls *load*. You can't put an airline seat into inventory and store it. That seat is as perishable as a box of raspberries. Hospitals face the same problem. You can't put a bed and all the equipment and highly trained personnel who staff a hospital into inventory. And every professional—lawyer, doctor, consultant—knows that her time can't be stored in inventory. The plot in most service businesses with high fixed costs turns on how to solve this problem.

It used to be that companies that made products operated with different economics. If you produced a widget, you could store that widget in inventory somewhere until a customer was ready to buy it. But in fast-moving product businesses, where customer tastes change rapidly, products are becoming as perishable as services. Kevin Rollins, vice chairman of Dell, says "We're in the vegetable business." What he means is that the technology is changing so fast that, if the company doesn't sell a computer as soon as it's made, it's likely to get stuck with a pile of obsolete machines. This insight about inventory and speed has driven over a decade of phenomenal performance at Dell. It is also why most CEOs now say that speed is one of their highest priorities no matter what business they're in.

Selling direct allowed Dell to run at a speed that has kept its competitors breathless for a decade. It has given Dell a direct link to its customers, and that link has given it better information about what customers want and when they will want it. Dell has used this information to forge partnerships with its suppliers that allow for just-in-time manufacture and delivery of components to Dell's assembly plants. As Michael Dell puts it, "We substitute information for inventory." That is better for Dell's suppliers, who can manufacture a steadier stream of components, and for Dell.

At first, other PC makers ignored Dell. Then, over the course of 15 years, one by one, they all more or less capitulated and joined Dell in selling direct. An entire business sector—the computer distributors who once controlled the PC business, representing over $75 billion in revenues in 2000—was left gasping for life. Three of the industry giants, CHS Electronics, MicroAge, and InaCom, all filed for Chapter 11 protection in 2000.

At one level, the moral of this story is simple: Offer customers a better deal and your business will grow. At another level, it is more complex: That better deal is created through a system, a business model built on an insight about value, which makes the better deal economically viable. Dell could offer customers more computer for less money because its *cost structure* (the term for an organization's total configuration of activities) resulted in lower costs.

What's next for Dell? As sales of personal computers began to slow, Dell shifted rapidly to products like servers, extending its direct model into new territory. The fact that the company has an explicit model, which all of its managers understand, helps Dell to adapt to change. That's not to say, however, that Dell's original model will endure for ever. The role of strategy—the subject of our next chapter—is to help management deal with that reality.

Stories that Change the World

Does a nonprofit organization need a business model? Absolutely. It may not use the term to describe its system for creating value. In fact, it probably doesn't. But like businesses, social enterprises are systems for creating value. A good business model, as we have seen, helps the people running an organization see the system as a coherent whole of interrelated parts. In the social sector, it serves the same function.

Look at any successful nonprofit or government agency, and you will find all the critical elements of a good business model: clearly drawn characters, with plausible motives, who come together in a plot that makes sense. The story always hinges on how the organization will change the world, or at least the specific aspect of the world its mission targets. Here, the twist in the plot—the critical insight about value—is what is sometimes called the organization's *theory of change*.

When William Bratton became New York's police commissioner in 1994, he had a very clear theory of change: Go after the petty, quality-of-life infractions like graffiti spraying and turnstile jumping and you will deter more serious crimes. In law enforcement circles this is known as the "broken-window" theory: When a broken window in a building isn't fixed immediately, people assume that no one cares and, soon, all the windows will be broken. Under Bratton, the NYPD showed that it cared. Its routine searches of quality-of-life offenders turned up hundreds of weapons that might have been used to commit more serious crimes. Operating from this simple, easy-to-communicate theory of change, Bratton was able to redirect the efforts of the NYPD, and serious crime in the city fell dramatically.

Elderhostel: A Fee-Based Model

For the nonprofit organization, the theory of change is its special insight about how it will fulfill its mission, how it will create social value. At the same time, its model must account for how it will gather all the resources it needs, whether it's by charging fees, raising funds, or attracting volunteers. Consider Elderhostel, an organization that has been changing the lives of older people for the past twenty-five years.

In the 1970s, American society was just beginning to grasp the implications of its rapidly increasing older population. What became known as "the graying of America" was not a pleasant prospect for most seniors. In the words of Elderhostel's founder, Marty Knowlton, growing old in America was a "wasteful, tragic process of disengagement." He believed the only way to change that process was for older people themselves to "realize their worth and become their own agents of change."

Elderhostel, which Knowlton founded with his colleague David Bianco in 1975, became a vehicle for that change. Its mission was to help older adults find new interests and enthusiasm through high quality, affordable, educational programs. Its founders were inspired by the European youth hostel movement, whose network of simple accommodations made it easy for adventurous young people to travel and meet each other. Why not use some of the college and university dorm rooms that stood empty part of the year to create something similar for older people?

Elderhostel's business model could hardly have been simpler. The "customer" was a retiree with lots of time, a flexible schedule, and a love of learning. Elderhostel's "products" were short courses provided by universities and other non-profit institutions such as museums. For the Elderhosteler, value was both the educational program and the sense of being part of a community of active and engaged people like themselves. That's the core of Elderhostel's theory of change.

How, then, does Elderhostel sustain what it does? Hostelers themselves cover most of the program costs through modest fees for tuition and accommodations. Keeping those fees affordable has always been a priority for Elderhostel, and its practices have been aligned around the theme of cost consciousness. The program providers all understand this, and it suits them because Elderhostel represents both an opportunity for public service and a chance to make better use of their facilities and generate some incremental income. Over time, some of the sites have found the business so attractive that they devote significant resources to the program.

Elderhostel grew rapidly, from a summer program for 220 in New Hampshire, to a worldwide movement with over two hundred thousand participants per year in fifty countries. That growth was fueled by satisfied customers and word-of-mouth referrals. The fact that Elderhostel didn't have to advertise was an important element in its low-cost, no-frills approach. Its major marketing expense has been a black-and-white book of course listings, reminiscent of *The Whole Earth Catalog*.

A generation later, Elderhostel is evolving along with its hostelers (who, on balance, are more vigorous and more prosperous than their predecessors) and with the booming market for educational and travel services specifically geared to mature adults. To stay relevant in what has become a crowded—and highly attractive—field, it is offering better accommodations and more travel-based and international programs. Clarity about its business model has helped Elderhostel to adapt to change without losing sight of its mission. Consider how Elderhostel has dealt with two issues, its pricing policy and the accommodations it offers.

Through the 1980s, all courses charged the same low fee—and many in the organization believed that one low price for all programs was sacred to Elderhostel's mission. However, that policy was preventing the organization from offering the richer variety of programs that Elderhostelers wanted and could afford. After a lot of soul searching, the tuition cap was abandoned in favor of a pricing policy that emphasizes good value rather than a specified low price. Now, a wider range of programs is offered at prices that reflect their cost. Eldehostel's management felt this change was in keeping with its story.

The question of upgrading accommodations was trickier. Most companies that offer packaged travel arrangements give customers a choice of accommodations at different prices with corresponding levels of amenities. Elderhostel decided instead to raise the comfort level across the board—the *hostel* part of its name is now a bit misleading. The accommodations for most programs are no longer the dorm-room, shared-bathroom style of the early years. What Elderhostel has not done—rightly given its business model and its theory of change—was to break up the sense of community by housing hostelers from one program in several different locations. Doing so would be out of character with Elderhostel's basic story.

City Year: Enlisting Donors and Volunteers

While largely self-supporting programs like Elderhostel's are becoming more common, most nonprofits rely on networks of donors and volunteers for the funds and resources they require. Consider the business model for City Year, an organization founded in Boston, in 1988, by Michael Brown and Alan Khazei, two young graduates of Harvard. City Year uses community service as the vehicle for youth development. It trains young people for what City Year defines as "the highest office in a democracy," citizenship, by having them work side by side for a year with people who come from different walks of life and ethnic backgrounds. Bringing diverse teams of kids together to work for a common purpose is the heart of City Year's theory of change. The year spent in service work teaches responsibility and social commitment. The team experience teaches diversity.

City Year, borrowing an idea from the Olympics, has found a natural ally in local companies who sponsor its teams. Doing so allows companies to support their communities in a visible way, not only with money, but through participation in citywide work days, during which local citizens work side by side with corps members to clean and rehabilitate public property and buildings. Consistent with its mission of engaged citizenship, at least 51 percent of City Year's budget is (and must be) privately funded.

Working from a clear theory of change and an understanding of what is and is not central to the model helps keep City Year's performance on track as it seeks to grow beyond its initial test site in Boston. People familiar with City Year might associate the organization with the red jackets its members wear, a visible symbol of the discipline the organization fosters in young people. When City Year tried to expand to a city in which red jackets were the uniform of a local gang, the organizers were stymied. Their original theory was that the red jackets were indispensable. Put to the test, however, they realized that matching jackets were essential to the bonding of the teams, but the color wasn't.

On the other hand, City Year will not bend on its diversity requirement. When one of the program's expansion sites was having trouble meeting this requirement, it sought an exemption so that it could move ahead. What it got was a team of experienced recruiters from Boston to help it meet the target. Diversity—mixing kids from every conceivable racial and ethnic group, from high-school dropouts to college graduates—has a direct effect on what the participants learn about themselves, about one another, and about how the world works. It is City Year's theory of change, its crucial insight about creating value. Without diversity there couldn't be any moving ahead, because there was no way to get the story right.

Chapter 3

Strategy: The Logic of Superior Performance

The essence of strategy is choosing what not to do.

—Michael E. Porter

Of all the concepts in management, strategy is the one that attracts the most attention and generates the most controversy. Almost everyone agrees that it is important. Almost no one agrees on what it is. Since the term was first applied to business enterprises in the late 1970s, there has been a steady stream of contending books and articles that seek to define strategy and specify how it should be developed. These definitions have encompassed everything from elaborate analytic exercises and five-year strategic plans, to companywide brainstorming sessions, to simple vision statements. It's not surprising that many people are skeptical of strategy.

But this is a concept you ignore at your peril. Strategy is critical to the performance of all organizations. Strategic thinking begins with a good business model that describes, as a system, the economic relationships central to fulfilling an organization's particular purpose. But strategy goes further because the business model does not factor in something that is omnipresent in the commercial world and growing fast in the social sector as well: competition. Sooner or later—and it is usually sooner—every enterprise runs into competitors. This chapter will explain how strategy deals with that reality, and what it means for an organization to achieve and sustain a competitive advantage.

As consumers, we choose among competing alternatives all the time. They may be as obvious and direct as the decision to buy a Ford instead of a Toyota or to invest in a mutual fund from Fidelity rather than Vanguard. Or they may be as subtle as the competition between a $500 Palm Pilot and a $5 notebook and pencil. There are always alternatives; and this is equally true for those who have capital and talent to invest. Unless you can promise superior returns or superior opportunities, the money and people needed to fuel an organization will go elsewhere. The same logic applies in the social sector, where many worthy causes compete for donors' funds and volunteers' time.

In a competitive world, doing a good job of creating value is only the necessary first step toward superior performance. Competition demands that you do a better job than the alternatives. And doing better, by definition, means being different. Organizations do better—they achieve superior performance—when they are unique, when they do something that no one else does in ways that no one else can duplicate. When you cut away all the jargon, this is what strategy is all about: how you are going to do better by being different.

The fundamental premise of doing better by being different is that you are playing in a world of alternatives. The strategic choices every enterprise makes, explicitly or implicitly, determine how it is positioned and configured in relation to those other alternatives. Broadly speaking, they are choices about which customers and markets to serve, what products and services to offer, and what kind of value to create. Made well, these strategic choices enable an enterprise to outperform its competitors.

Doing Better by Being Different

In 1962, the owner of a small string of Ben Franklin variety stores opened the first Wal*Mart in Rogers, Arkansas (population 4,500). By the end of the twentieth century, the company Sam Walton founded was operating some four thousand stores and serving 100 million customers. It employed more than one million people, and was poised to overtake General Motors as number one on the Fortune 500 list of the world's largest companies. In the twenty years leading up to Sam's death in 1992, Wal*Mart achieved a twenty-year average return on equity of 33 percent, and a compound average sales growth of 35 percent. Over the years, many managers and hourly employees have retired as millionaires, thanks to a profit-sharing plan that includes everyone who works twenty or more hours a week for at least a year. This is superior performance by anyone's standard. How did Walton and his associates do it?

Discount retailing emerged as a new business model in the mid-1950s, when a slew of industry pioneers (now long forgotten) began to apply supermarket logic to the sale of general merchandise. Supermarkets had been educating customers since the 1930s about the value of exchanging personal service for lower food prices. Now, those consumers could become central characters in another innovative business story.

A new breed of retailers saw they could adapt the basic story line of the supermarket to clothing, appliances, and a host of other consumer goods. The idea was to offer lower prices than conventional department stores did, by slashing costs. Thus, the basic business model for discount retailing took shape. First, strip away the department store's physical amenities, the carpeting, and the chandeliers; second, configure the stores to handle large volumes efficiently; and third, have fewer salespeople on the floor and rely on customers to serve themselves. Do all of these things well, and you could offer low prices and still make money.

Walton heard about the new discount stores, visited a few and liked their potential. In 1962, he decided to set out on his own, borrowing a lot of ideas for his early stores from Kmart and others. But it was what he chose to do differently—the ways he put his own stamp on the basic business model—that made Wal*Mart so fabulously successful and ultimately allowed it to run rings around the competition.

How did Sam position Wal*Mart to make it different from other discounters? From the very start, Walton chose to serve a different group of customers in a different set of markets. The ten largest discounters in 1962, all gone today, focused on large metropolitan areas and cities like New York. Wal*Mart's key strategy in Sam's own words, "was to put good-sized stores into little one-horse towns which everybody else was ignoring." He sought out isolated rural towns with populations between five thousand and twenty-five thousand. Herein lies the difference between a model and a strategy. His model (discount retailing) was the same as Kmart's. His strategy was unique.

Sam was a small-town guy himself, and knew the terrain well. The nearest city was probably a four-hour drive. Sam rightly bet that if his stores could match or beat those city prices, people would shop at home. Moreover, many of Wal*Mart's markets were too small to support more than one large retailer. So, by being first, Sam was able to preempt competitors and discourage them from entering Wal*Mart's territory. (Strategists call this a *first-mover advantage*, and it has been a kind of holy grail for e-commerce entrepreneurs, who have tried to stake out similarly exclusive territories in cyberspace. It's important to understand that being a first mover is an advantage only when there is a real entry barrier to deter other players from moving in.) At the same time, Sam never abused his position as the only store in town; he never fell into the trap of taking his customers for granted. Wal*Mart has made a practice of regularly refreshing and upgrading older stores, so that they continue to appeal to customers despite the lure of newer competitors.

Wal*Mart also took a different approach to merchandising and pricing—that is, it promised customers a different kind of value. While competitors relied heavily on private-label goods, second-tier brands, and special price promotions, Wal*Mart promised national brands at everyday low prices. What made this promise more than a marketing slogan was Wal*Mart's systematic pursuit of efficiency and low cost.

Everything Wal*Mart does supports its ability to make good on its promise of value. Everyday low pricing, for example, means Wal*Mart spends far less on advertising circulars than its rivals who have to publicize their frequent, special promotions. (According to one comparative study, for example, Wal*Mart's ten to fifteen circulars per year stacked up against fifty to 100 for its rivals.) There are similar costs savings all along Wal*Mart's value chain, in just about every activity required to manage a store and its *supply chain* (how the company purchases goods and transports them to its stores). Much as the Japanese broke the old auto industry tradeoff between cost and quality by redesigning both purchasing and manufacturing, so Wal*Mart has brought its own version of the quality revolution to retailing.

Much of that revolution was embodied in the person of Sam Walton himself. He watched expenses like a hawk, making frugality and continuous cost reduction a way of life. On buying trips, for instance, he believed that expenses should not exceed 1 percent of the cost of the items purchased. So, even though he was one of the world's richest men, he'd often walk instead of taking a cab, or double up in a hotel room to stay within budget. Such stories became legends within Wal*Mart, setting a standard of behavior throughout the organization. Wal*Mart people are known for such penny-saving practices as calling vendors collect. Its negotiations with suppliers are notorious both for where they take place (windowless cubicles at headquarters in Bentonville, Arkansas), and for Wal*Mart's ability to drive a tough bargain.

Tight as Sam was, he invested early and heavily in systems to speed the flow of information throughout the company. Information technology may be just about the only area in which Wal*Mart has historically outspent competitors. That's because, in retailing, timely information is the key to maximizing sales and minimizing costs. The better your information about what's selling and what's not, store by store, the better you can avoid the twin perils of retailing—too little inventory or too much. When you run out of merchandise that people want to buy, you lose a sale. When you have too much merchandise, you have to mark down the price in order to get rid of it, hurting your profit margins.

Wal*Mart set the pace for its industry in information technology—whether it was the use of handheld scanners (as early as 1983) to price goods and track inventory, transmitting data daily from each store to the head office, or linking electronically to key suppliers like P&G (years before the Internet) so that they could replenish stores and warehouses in response to real-time sales information. The result was that both Wal*Mart and its suppliers had the benefit of lower inventory costs and higher sales.

Logistics also became a key factor in Wal*Mart's ability to deliver low prices, thanks, in part, to the geographic strategy the company pursued. As it expanded, Wal*Mart grew from the inside out, clustering its stores so that each was within easy delivery distance of a centrally located warehouse. This hub-and-spoke system allowed Wal*Mart to supply stores frequently (sometimes as often as several times a week), reducing inventory costs and stockouts. It also lowered shipping costs because the great majority of the company's trucks traveled full.

As Wal*Mart kept finding new ways to improve efficiency, the concept of storing goods in warehouses gave way to a radically different notion, moving goods through distribution centers. One of the breakthroughs in this transformation was the process Wal*Mart pioneered called *cross-docking*. Goods from a supplier's truck went seamlessly from an unloading dock directly into a truck bound for the stores. The goal was just what the name implies: to get goods into the stores without ever unpacking them—let alone allowing them to sit in storage.

Wal*Mart's strategy—quality goods for less—is easy to articulate. It's a lot harder to execute, of course. Execution is enormously important to an organization's performance, as you'll see in later chapters, and Wal*Mart is as superb an executor as ever you'll find. The key to its superior performance, however, has been its strategy. Only by being different could Wal*Mart have created enormous value for its customers and, at the same time, captured substantial value for its owners. The next section will explain why that is so.

The Link Between Strategy and Performance

As common—and overused—as the word *strategy* is today, its origin as a management term is remarkably recent. Peter Drucker's 1964 book, *Managing for Results,* was originally titled *Business Strategies*. This title was rejected, however, after both author and publisher did some informal test marketing of the idea. In the Preface to a later edition of the book, Drucker explains why. "'Strategy,' we were told again and again, 'belongs to military or perhaps to political campaigns but not to business.'"

In war and politics, the aim of strategy is clear. Strategy is about winning the battle, the war, the election. One side, and only one, will prevail. The other side will be defeated. This is what strategists call a *zero-sum* game. Any victory for A is necessarily a defeat for B.

Strategy in management is also about winning. Unlike wars or elections, however, competition is not always a zero-sum game. In business and in the social sector there is room for more than one winner. Superior performance doesn't require the annihilation of an enemy. Wal*Mart is a winner in the discount retailing game, for example, but so is Target, which has chosen to create value for customers by focusing on style and fashion. The losers in the industry—the chronic underperformers like Kmart throughout the 1990s—are companies that try to be all things to all people. They fail to find distinctive ways to compete.

Strategy is something of an art as well as a science, and we will discuss what makes it so hard in a minute. But the underlying logic of business strategy couldn't be simpler. A company's profits are what's left after subtracting costs from revenues. It follows, then, that there are only two ways one company can outperform another. It can get its customers to pay higher prices or it can operate on lower costs. To do either of those two things, it has to be different—or how else could you explain its ability to charge more or to use fewer resources? That's the simple arithmetic of superior performance.

Without a strategy that in some way makes what you do unique, you may create lots of value, but competition will prevent you from charging higher prices, so you will turn most if not all of that value over to consumers. That is, you may be able to create value, but you won't be able to capture any of it. That's what happened, for example, to the dairy farmers who adopted "bovine somatotropin," a hormone that increases milk yields by as much as 20 percent. The early adopters initially made more money, because, for a while, prices held steady while their costs per gallon were falling. But as more farmers jumped on the bandwagon, the increased supply of milk lowered the price for everyone—which was good for consumers, bad for the dairy farmers.

A more complex version of this story explains what has happened to the consumer electronics industry. In the 1980s, competition from Japan was every western CEO's worst nightmare.

Whether it was TVs, VCRs, or fax machines, Japan's ability to produce high-quality products at low cost drove U.S. and European competitors out of those businesses. Since then, Japan has floundered for more than a decade. Why? A big piece of the answer is poor strategy. So many Japanese companies competed by imitating each other in every dimension—serving the same customers, with the same products—that they achieved the business equivalent of a pyrrhic victory. As a group, they won the battle in consumer electronics. But they won in a way that destroyed their ability to make money.

Competition in consumer electronics is intense, approaching what economists refer to as *perfect competition*, in which equally matched rivals face off head to head. Under perfect competition, switching costs are low, which means there is little to prevent a customer from switching from product A to product B, if B offers a better deal. Entry barriers are low, as well, which means there is little to prevent a new competitor from entering the business. There is more than a touch of irony in the language here. What's perfect for an economist is perfect only for customers. For managers and workers it is a nightmare. They are more likely to call this form of competition *cut-throat*. Lots of rivals vie with each other, and plentiful supply keeps prices and wages down.

In perfect competition, as soon as one company comes up with a new or improved way to do something, or lowers prices, everyone else must quickly match the move or fall behind. It's like running a neverending race that no one can win. That was the case for the dairy farmers, and it was true in the first wave of e-commerce. As soon as one e-tailer offered free delivery, for example, others immediately matched the offer. When more and more Internet service providers entered the market, the price of monthly service steadily fell from more than $20 to $15 to $10 to $0. This is why economists say that in perfect competition, profits tend to be "bid away." Perfect competition is a kind of buyer's paradise, resulting in better products and lower prices, while producers, unable to differentiate themselves, struggle to make a profit and stay in business.

At the other end of the competitive spectrum is monopoly. Here, one player has not merely differentiated itself, it has acquired a stranglehold on a product or service for which there are no alternatives. When telephone service could only come into your home through a wire, and physical constraints dictated that there could be only one wire, telephone service was a monopoly. The same was true for public utilities like electricity and water. Left unregulated, a monopoly has enormous power to impose very high prices relative to its costs. That's why government steps in to protect consumers from potential abuses, and to redress the power imbalance by setting prices or breaking up the monopoly.

The line between a wildly successful business that plays by the rules and an abuser of monopoly power can be a difficult one to draw—as protracted legal battles, such as the case brought by the U.S. Department of Justice against Microsoft, reveal. Whether Microsoft used its market power unfairly to keep competitors out of its markets is a legal question. Whatever the legal answer, it is undeniably clear that Microsoft's Windows operating system has become so dominant that, for a time at least, and for most customers, there were no practical alternatives. As a result, Microsoft has been able to set prices dramatically higher than its costs and, throughout the 1990s, to capture unprecedented value for its owners.

Few organizations compete at either end of the spectrum. Few are as completely undifferentiated (*perfect competition*) or as unique (*monopoly*). Yet it's helpful to keep the spectrum in mind because it allows us to visualize an important aspect of competition and what strategy aims to do. Business executives are society's leading champions of free markets and competition, words that, for them, evoke a world view and value system that rewards good ideas and hard work, and that fosters innovation and meritocracy. Truth be told, the competition every manager longs for is a lot closer to Microsoft's end of the spectrum than it is to the dairy farmers'. All the talk about the virtues of competition notwithstanding, the aim of business strategy is to move an enterprise away from perfect competition and in the direction of monopoly. Warren Buffett, the legendary investor, who describes his company, Berkshire Hathaway, as a "castle of capital," put it this way in remarks cited in the *New York Times*. "Other people want to take our castle away. . . . I reward my managers for building a moat around our castle and then making the moat deeper, wider and filling it with alligators."

Sam Walton would have approved. Recall his first and key strategy: locating his stores in markets that other discounters ignored. Initially, Walton competed by not competing, literally going where the competition wasn't. His moat, in other words, was hundreds of miles wide. And even as Wal*Mart's inexorable geographic expansion led the company into markets served by its rivals, it continued to do better, in part because it avoided head-to-head competition. Well into the 1990s, only 55 percent of Wal*Mart's stores competed directly with a Kmart, whereas 82 percent of Kmart's stores faced direct competition from Wal*Mart. Moreover, by the time Walton had to face direct competition, he had found the alligators he needed and staked out a distinct value positioning for the chain. Smart competitors like Sam Walton know that the best competition is no competition.

How Do You Play the Game of Strategy?

If the game of strategy is about being and staying different, how is it played? In recent years, many business leaders and thinkers have argued that technological change combined with ever-larger, more dynamic markets has made the notion of a sustainable competitive advantage—of staying different—obsolete. There's some truth to that, but only some.

Compared to the business world of twenty-five years ago,

there is certainly more truth now in Intel Chairman Andy Grove's widely quoted dictum, "only the paranoid survive." Even the most settled and seemingly mature industries (such as banking, telecommunications, and utilities) have been shaken up and transformed. Former giants have disappeared, and new competitors have captured their castles. At the end of the day, however, winners sustain their superior performance for many years at a stretch—in fact, decades—and they do so by creating value in ways that competitors cannot copy.

The game may be moving faster, and the advantages may be shorter lived, but the objective is the same: figuring out how to hide from competition, or dampen it, or constrain it, so that you can earn superior returns. David Pottruck, co-CEO of Schwab, acknowledges both the quicker pace of competition and its heightened intensity. What do you do when you don't have a moat? Pottruck quipped. "I keep trying to move the castle." In other words, he has to find a new way to differentiate his offering.

Both approaches to strategy—building a moat or moving the castle—create obstacles to perfect competition. Both are ways that organizations make what they do unique rather than a commodity. Both mean erecting entry barriers to deter competitors, and raising switching costs to hang on to customers. Strategy asks how you can differentiate what you do, or how you do it, so that in fact or in perception customers believe there is no substitute for it.

Remember the old secret formulas that advertisers used to trumpet? While these were often nothing more than sales pitches, in some industries (such as pharmaceuticals), there really are secret formulas, which are legally protected by company patents. A patented drug is, in fact, a legal monopoly granted by the government, and it should therefore come as no surprise that the pharmaceuticals industry consistently outpaces almost all others in its financial results, or that the cost of prescription medicines is a growing political problem. (Most countries, other than the United

States, solve the problem by regulating prices, which is why the same drug costs more in the United States than it does in, say, Canada or France.) Patents are an extreme form of what every business wants to do, which is to prevent the competition from copying what it does.

If a patent is a roadblock to competition, a brand is at least a speed bump. Companies invest hundreds of millions of dollars in creating brand identity, in order to reduce the likelihood that customers will switch to someone else offering them a similar product and/or a lower price. They create loyalty programs to reward frequent flyers or frequent buyers.

In the industrial economy, the barriers to perfect competition were often physical—the wire or pipeline that ran to your house, for instance, or the huge plant required to manufacture a product. In the knowledge economy, the barriers are shifting increasingly to intangibles, such as intellectual property or the know-how embodied in a company's core competences in areas such as new product development or customer service.

Making Strategic Tradeoffs

One of the most effective roadblocks to pure competition is a unique positioning. When this positioning involves tradeoffs, it is likely to have real staying power as well. *Tradeoffs* are the strategic equivalent of a fork in the road, where taking one path means that you cannot simultaneously take the other. Enterprise Rent-A-Car provides a simple example of how this works.

If you walk into the car rental section of any good-sized airport, you're sure to see counters for Avis and Hertz, as well as a host of smaller rivals. But you won't see Enterprise, which has historically been more profitable than its better-known competitors, despite the fact that its rates are about 30 percent lower. What explains this difference? And why don't Hertz and Avis do the same things Enterprise does? In a word, *tradeoffs*.

Unlike Hertz and Avis, who target air travelers, Enterprise has built its business around the person whose own car is in the shop. For this set of customers, price is likely to matter if they're paying for the rental themselves, and it's sure to matter if their insurance company is paying. So, Enterprise has designed its operation to eliminate everything that would add cost without also increasing the customer's willingness to pay. For example, Enterprise stores its fleet in cheap suburban lots instead of paying for expensive airport real estate. It keeps its cars in service longer than its rivals do. It spends less on advertising, because its customers mostly come via referrals from insurance appraisers and repair shops.

Enterprise's superior performance is the result of all these choices. Although its customers pay less than its competitors' customers do, its cost savings more than compensate for the discount. Those savings result not from doing more efficiently the same things its rivals do, but from choosing a different *cost structure*, the unique configuration of activities tailored to Enterprise's strategy. As for Hertz and Avis, while, in theory, they could copy some of Enterprise's practices, it would be hard for them to do so without compromising the value they create for the customers whom they have chosen.

Dell Computer offers another good illustration of the way that tradeoffs make it hard for rivals with a different positioning to copy what you do. Positioning tradeoffs sustained Dell's superior performance for well over a decade, allowing Dell to make money in personal computers, even when other PC companies were awash in red ink. As we saw in the previous chapter, Dell's direct model ultimately became the way that the entire industry did business. Why didn't Dell's competitors respond more quickly? Why did the other computer makers allow Dell to capture so much of the industry's value for so long?

The simple answer is that Dell's rivals were trapped by their own strategies. If they tried to sell direct, like Dell, they would disrupt their existing distribution channels and alienate the resellers on whom they relied. So, for years, Dell's rivals were damned if they copied Dell and damned if they didn't. Managing a hybrid system, in which some PCs were built to order and some to inventory, is both complicated and costly. Manufacturers that tried to straddle the two different ways of doing business were likely to end up with more inventory, higher costs of obsolescence, and more writeoffs.

One of the basic rules of competitive strategy is that where there are real tradeoffs, you can't have it both ways. Dell discovered this for itself, in 1989, when, thinking its direct business wouldn't grow fast enough, it tried to sell through retailers. It retreated almost immediately, however, when it realized just how badly the move would damage its performance. The problem is that if you can have it both ways, everyone else can too. Your way of being different must have staying power—your castle needs a moat—or your performance will be undistinguished.

Thinking Strategically

What makes strategy especially hard is that no organization acts in a vacuum. While you are excavating your moat, someone else across town or across the globe may be working on a new catapult, or even a cannon. Thinking strategically means recognizing that the world is filled with purposeful people whose aims may constrain or challenge yours. A lumberjack, deciding how to split a log, can reasonably expect that the log won't fight back. A general trying to take out an enemy's position, on the other hand, had better expect resistance to his plans.

Strategic thinking is necessarily interactive: It acknowledges that the world is filled with potential rivals and allies; it allows for both competition and cooperation. This approach to strategic thinking dates to the middle of the twentieth century, when mathematician John von Neumann and economist Oskar Morgenstern wrote the *Theory of Games and Economic Behavior*. (Game theory was recognized with a Nobel Prize in 1994, when John Harsanyi, John Nash, and Reinhard Selten shared the economics prize for their work in this field.)

From the theoreticians of game theory, managers have learned some important lessons about strategic thinking. First, every move will evoke a response. To understand what might happen, you have to imagine all the other players' possible moves, then factor in your reaction to theirs, and so on. The objective is to look forward into the game, then reason back to decide which course of action is most likely to help you end up where it is you want to be. Second, in economic games, it's critical to keep your eye on the whole value chain—and on the value that each player adds to the whole. Follow that trail and it will lead you to see who is likely to have the power to do what. Third, although the key to success in a game would seem to be focusing on your own position, in practice, the opposite holds true. You have to put yourself in the shoes— and even the minds—of the other players.

A skirmish in the larger war between Pepsi and Coke illustrates these lessons at work. In the 1970s, Pepsi's market research told it that customers would value lighter-weight packaging, hence the switch from glass bottles to plastic. Of course, Coke could copy Pepsi's move but, at the time, Coke's uniquely shaped glass bottle was its icon. Coke had spent hundreds of millions of dollars, over decades of advertising and promotion, to establish that image in consumers' minds. Copying Pepsi would thus be a very costly thing for Coke to do. Pepsi found a move that would create value for its customers at the same time that it destroyed value for Coke.

This kind of strategic thinking—looking forward in the game—is essential to creating strategies with real staying power. It does no good, after all, to stake out a unique position if others can easily copy what you've done, or if someone can offer a better alternative. In chapter 1, we talked about a fledgling company called OnTimeAuditor.com with its easy-to-understand value creation for customers. Now, suppose you were running the company or thinking about investing in its stock, that is, suppose you had a stake in this company's performance. What would you want to know about the company's strategy?

First, if they demonstrate that there's money to be made here, would it be easy for someone else to duplicate this service? (In other words, do they face the threat of new entrants?) If so, what will prevent their customers from switching to another provider? Could customers create their own software and do it themselves? Are some customers going to be better for them than others, more likely to stick with them? Should they focus on trying to lock them in before other competitors arise? Should they target smaller to midsize companies for whom doing this themselves is apt to be too much trouble? Or, should they go after big companies for whom the payoff will be larger?

Another set of critical questions would revolve around how the shippers will respond. OnTimeAuditor.com hasn't found a better way to manage shipping, remember. It hasn't taken cost out of the system, as Dell did by eliminating the middleman. What it has found is a way to give its customers greater power over their suppliers (the shippers) by providing them with information. In essence, the company is transferring value from the shipper to the customer and taking a fee in the bargain. Are FedEx and UPS likely to sit back and do nothing as millions of dollars slip through their fingers? Probably not. But, what will they do?

The shippers might simply raise their prices to cover the new costs, or they might eliminate or relax their service guarantees. Both solutions are feasible and likely if the balance of power between the shippers and their customers tilts in favor of the shippers—if, that is, the customers don't defect to some better alternative if prices rise. The shippers' response will also depend on the level of competition among them. All might move in the same direction, or one or more might use this as an opportunity to try to lure new customers away from a rival.

If the big, established shippers are able to pass the higher costs on to their customers then, ironically, OnTimeAuditor.com may have a future. Why ironically? Because the value created by the refunds will probably be offset by the higher prices. Alternatively, this threat may spur the shippers to improve the quality of their service, which is often how competition drives innovation and value creation. It may push them to figure out how to use information themselves to reduce the number of late deliveries. If this is the case, OnTimeAuditor.com will be in trouble. The catch-22 of this business, and many others, is that as long as it's not too successful, it is more likely to succeed. Big profits will surely attract the attention of potential rivals ("there's easy money to be made here") and of the shippers themselves ("we can't afford to let these guys eat our lunch").

OnTimeAuditor.com is a very simple business idea, and as clean an example of value creation as you'd hope to find. However, once you start to think about value capture, the story turns out to be not so simple after all. Strategy is difficult, because it is about how others will react to what you do. Even with a simple business like this one, there are many players on the board—not to mention the potential players who have yet to appear. And these players are ordinary people, mere mortals who make decisions for all sorts of reasons that are neither predictable nor even rational. The counterbalance to all these uncertainties and unknowns is a disciplined way of thinking, built on an understanding of the basic economic forces at work, to varying degrees, in all competitive situations. First introduced by Michael Porter in 1979, the so-called *five forces* model has since become a foundation of the strategy field. Porter identified the underlying forces that determine the attractiveness of any industry: the competition among existing players, the threat of new entrants, the power of suppliers, the power of customers, and the availability of substitute products.

It is the interplay of these forces that determines where on the spectrum of competition—from perfect competition to monop-oly—an industry is likely to be. It is within or against the play of these forces that every organization first attempts to dig its moat and fill it with alligators and, second, to fend off assaults that may come from all sides at once (as our questions about OnTimeAudi-tor.com illustrate).

Patents and proprietary intellectual property, brands, and spe-cial competencies help defend the castle, while strategy creates the protective moat that underlies the superior performance of organi-zations like Dell, Wal*Mart, and Enterprise. But sooner or later, if the prize is worth the battle, someone will find a way to assault your castle. The more open and innovative markets become, the more al-ternatives customers have. In myriad ways, the new economy is forcing the old to be more responsive, to move its castles. Some call it "Internet anxiety," the sense that some upstart will upend your business (as Amazon did to book selling, and E*Trade and Ameri-trade did to Wall Street brokerage firms like Merrill Lynch).

Detroit's planned obsolescence worked for a long time, forcing customers to buy new cars because their old ones were designed not to last. Then, competition from Toyota and Honda forced dramatic innovation in the auto industry. Similarly, the planned inconve-nience of shopping malls has been under attack from competing re-tail formats, both other park-and-shop models like the big-box retailers, and the web's point-and-click models. Shoppers like it when competing stores are clustered, so that they can comparison shop. Mall design deliberately thwarted them, forcing people to walk past a lot of shops. Many frustrated, time-pressed shoppers defected to more convenient alternatives. Now that malls aren't the only game in town, they will have to innovate if they want to survive.

From Doing Good to Doing Better: Strategy for Nonprofits

Once, nonprofit organizations appeared to operate in a parallel universe, largely untouched by the pressures of competition and markets. People joined nonprofits to do good, to serve, not to compete. There's a wonderful (although probably apocryphal) story often told about the Special Olympics that captures this spirit. The disabled contestants at the starting line are poised to compete in the 100-yard dash. At the starting gun, they move forward as best they can, but one entrant stumbles, and begins to cry. One by one, the others hear him. Each one pauses, then stops, and turns back to comfort the fallen runner. All join, arm in arm, and move forward as one to the finish line.

The moral of the story, of course, is that helping others is more important than winning—that true winning is, in fact, about helping others, not beating them. This ethic of service is deeply ingrained in most nonprofits, but the emergence of competition everywhere has left many in the social sector feeling that it is under attack. David Lawrence, chairman and CEO of Kaiser Permanente, the nation's largest nonprofit health-care organization, describes the new climate, and the fundamental question it has raised for many in the social sector: "Events of the last decade provoked organizational 'midlife crises' for many mission-driven organizations, including Kaiser Permanente. Was it possible to compete in the marketplace and, at the same time, remain true to our social mission?"

It is a critical question and, as Lawrence himself goes on to argue, a false tradeoff. Strategy properly understood as doing better by being different is not at odds with the sense of mission that animates nonprofit organizations. On the contrary, strategy is the key to achieving mission. The goal of strategy—superior performance versus competing alternatives—is desperately needed in a world where the demand for many social-sector services is so great, unhappily, that the prospect of an oversupply is kind of a bad joke. In a world of scarce resources, we need the greatest social return for every dollar we spend, whether it is on literacy or homelessness or the environment.

Much as the strategy of a business explains how it will do better by being different, a nonprofit's strategy explains how its unique approach will achieve better results for society. Just as no business can succeed by trying to be all things to all people, so, too, must nonprofit organizations make critical choices about what they will do and, just as important, what they *won't* do.

Consider The Nature Conservancy, one of the largest conservation organizations in the world, and one with a remarkably clear and consistent strategy. Since its founding in 1951, TNC has had a clear mission, "to preserve plants and animals and special habitats that represent the diversity of life." It has also operated with an explicit theory of change. The Nature Conservancy fulfills its mission of saving threatened habitats and species by buying and setting aside land. What it *doesn't* do, is engage in advocacy as many other environmental groups do.

The money to buy the land comes from individual donors. TNC has specifically targeted those donors for whom protected landscapes are a valuable product. Says John Sawhill, its former CEO, TNC aims its appeal to the "growing segment of people who love the outdoors and want to preserve it—and who are looking for groups that are achieving tangible results. They like the fact that we use private-sector techniques to achieve our objectives, that we protect the environment the old-fashioned way: We buy it." What TNC *doesn't* do, and consciously so, is become dependent on government funding.

The Nature Conservancy, then, positions itself against the alternatives with which it competes for funds as a private organization, financed privately, using free-market techniques. Sawhill describes the positioning this way: "We think of ourselves as Adam Smith with a green thumb." Morever, TNC deliberately takes a positive, nonconfrontational, good-news approach, which is consistent with its overall strategy. For example, they report to donors on the growing number of acres they have preserved.

What TNC *doesn't* do, as many environmental groups do, is to try to spur people to action by forcing them to confront unpleasant realities.

At the end of the day, TNC achieves superior performance by making clear and consistent choices that follow logically from its mission and its strategy. Like all good strategies, those choices involve *tradeoffs*, those forks in the road we described earlier. With a clear grasp of its mission, TNC has developed a strategy that makes it unique, and that makes it clear when to say no to actions that would cause the organization to lose its focus and squander its resources.

Staying the course is difficult for any organization. For businesses, the challenge most often is growth. The pressure to grow can lead organizations to extend themselves too broadly, to blur their positioning, and, thus, to damage their performance. New initiatives are added piecemeal with the idea that each one will contribute new revenues. Over time, however, the whole can become less than the sum of its parts.

In the social sector, this loss of focus is sometimes referred to as *mission creep*. Sometimes, it comes from within, from the natural desire to address needs that feel related to the organization's mission, but which may stretch it beyond its ability to be effective. Habitat for Humanity, for example, has a wonderful model for building homes within stable communities, where people with roots in the community—local merchants, volunteers, the future homeowner—all join in a grassroots effort. Should Habitat extend its efforts to urban homelessness or disaster relief? True, these are areas of great need that involve housing, but do they fit Habitat's theory of change, its business model, and the strategy that makes it unique?

Most often, mission creep in the social sector occurs when organizations pursue funding from well-intentioned donors who want to support initiatives that don't fit the organization's strategy.

When a substantial donor offers a cash-strapped organization money that is off mission, it is very hard—but critically important—to say *no*. John Sawhill explains why The Nature Conservancy turned down several hundred thousand dollars to start a program on population. "You always must ask," says Sawhill, "'Given our limited resources and the enormous challenges we face, how will this advance our mission of protecting biodiversity?' We often have to say no to projects that, however tantalizing, are tangential to our goals."

Chapter 4

Organization: Where to Draw the Lines

*We trained hard . . . but every time we were beginning to form
into teams, we would be reorganized. I was to learn later in life
that we tend to meet new situations by reorganizing . . . and a
wonderful method it can be for creating the illusion of progress
while producing confusion, inefficiency, and demoralization.*

—Petronius Arbiter
Satyricon (first century A.D.)

Organization isn't a buzzword, but the simple question "What
should an organization look like?" has probably spawned more
buzzwords—and caused more dislocation in people's lives—than
any other management topic. Over the past two decades, most
major enterprises have undergone some form of radical reorganization, restructuring, or reengineering, with many (including
giants like AT&T and IBM) undergoing more than one. What
makes these changes confusing, as well as disruptive, is that they
seem to be pulling in opposite directions at once.

On the one hand, the prevailing bias is decidedly against big-
ness, and anything that might stifle the entrepreneurial spirit.
Practices such as outsourcing, free agency, and strategic partner-

ships have become the most popular ways to make organizations lighter by redefining what's inside and what's outside their boundaries. Big organizations have been delayering and downsizing—shedding people, in other words—and they've been spinning off whole functions and business units in order to become leaner, faster, and more focused. Increasingly, value creation is happening across company borders.

At the same time, however, we are in the midst of the largest wave of mergers and acquisitions in the history of business. The icon of competitiveness and good management is a huge conglomerate named GE which, under Jack Welch's leadership, bought hundreds of other companies. Cisco Systems, one of the great success stories of the post-PC era, had such a voracious appetite for companies with promising technology that being acquired by Cisco became the dream of many startups. New corporate names tell the story: DaimlerChrysler, ExxonMobil, AOL Time Warner. For the record, everyone extols the virtues of being small and virtual yet, in fact, companies that were already big are getting even bigger.

This chapter explains why organizational lines are drawn—and then redrawn—as they are. Management's job, turning complexity and specialization into performance, requires it to draw three different kinds of lines. First, the *boundary lines*, which separate what's inside and what's outside. Second, the *lines of the organization chart*, which map how the whole is divided into working units and how each part relates to the others. Third are the sometimes invisible, but always important, *lines of authority*. These determine who gets to decide what, and how the internal game is played.

How should companies organize? Where should the lines be drawn? Bigger or smaller? Focused or diversified? Centralized or decentralized? Top down or bottom up? Is it better to own and control assets and employees, or to string together networks of partners and freelancers? Why do we seem, when it comes to these questions, to be changing our minds all the time, constantly redrawing the lines?

The answer is this: The design of an organization is implicit in its strategy, so much so that it's sometimes hard to tell where strategy leaves off and organization begins. Because strategy is dynamic, organizations must be flexible. Drawing the lines of organization is an ongoing struggle to stay relevant, not a job done once and for all.

More than anything else, where the lines are drawn depends on what the organization is trying to accomplish, on how it is trying to do better by being different. A clear strategy thus becomes a kind of blueprint for an organization's design, shaping the most basic decisions about its scale (how big must we be?), its scope (how far should our offerings and activities extend?), and its structure (how should we organize ourselves?). Drawing the lines of organization is the concrete answer to those questions.

Ford *versus* Sloan: Two Strategies, Two Structures

The battle for dominance in the automobile industry offers a classic illustration of the link between strategy and organization. The story begins a century ago, with Henry Ford. Within a few years of founding the Ford Motor Company in 1903, Ford's ambition had crystallized: he would build a motorcar for the multitudes, a car that every working man could afford. "Crazy Henry," as his neighbors called him, was bucking the conventional wisdom of his day. Motorcars were rich men's toys, fun, but expensive and unreliable. Car making was a craft; vehicles were made by hand, one at a time.

After years of obsessive tinkering, Ford created the car of his dreams. Sturdy and easy to drive, the Model T was priced at $825. In its first year, 1908, over ten thousand were sold. That was just the beginning. Ford kept chipping away at costs. By 1912, he was able to sell the Model T for only $575. It was the first time the price of a car was lower than the average annual wage. By 1913, sales had soared to nearly a quarter of a million cars.

Ford's purpose gave rise to his strategy and his strategy dictated the structure, scale, and scope of his organization. Ford's motorcar for the multitude had to be affordable, which meant economies of scale and mass production. The cheaper the Model T became, the more people could afford them. And the more Model T's people bought, the cheaper each one became.

The breakthrough innovation—the one responsible for the 30 percent price drop between 1908 and 1912—was the assembly line. Ford was inspired by the disassembly lines he had observed in Chicago's meat packing plants, where automated trolleys carried the carcasses over the heads of the butchers, so that each could make his designated cut. The assembly line gave Ford a decisive productivity advantage over his rivals. By 1914, Ford made more than 260,000 cars with 13,000 workers. The rest of the industry combined turned out roughly 287,000 cars, about 10 percent more than Ford, but used over five times the numbers of workers— some 66,000—to do so.

Limiting the scope of his product line to one model made Ford's dream possible. Every part and process was analyzed, subdivided into its simplest components, and standardized to maximize efficiency and minimize cost. The result was a highly specialized production system that could do only one thing, but it did that thing very, very well.

The organization that matched Ford's strategy was the epitome of command and control. Every detail was designed from the top down, and managed through a hierarchical, centralized organization with Mr. Ford himself issuing orders. There was no doubt in the Ford Motor Company about where the lines of authority were drawn.

In 1920, there was a recession, and demand for cars fell.

Because Ford's costs were so low, he was able to drop his price by 25 percent. General Motors couldn't afford to match Ford, and its sales plummeted. By 1921, Ford had 55 percent of the market. All the General Motors brands, combined, had just 11 percent.

Sloan Strikes Back

In the same year that Henry Ford launched the Model T, William C. Durant, then head of Buick, formed the General Motors Company by acquiring a string of independent car and component makers. After companies such as Cadillac and Chevrolet were acquired, they continued to go their own ways, however, competing as much against each other as they did against Ford. Durant assembled the pieces we recognize as General Motors, but never figured out how to turn them into a working whole.

That job fell to his better-known successor, Alfred Sloan. In the early 1920s, Sloan knew he couldn't compete head to head with Ford's low-cost Model T. But what if he positioned Chevrolet as more than basic transportation? By adding, as standard, features such as a starter, GM could price the Chevrolet above the Ford and still claim to be giving the customer "more for the dollar." Moreover, GM could work systematically up the socioeconomic ladder, offering "a car for every purse and purpose." Product variety and customer segmentation was Sloan's strategy for GM.

Sloan had the right idea, but positioning each GM brand to meet the needs of a different customer was easier said than done. It required a radical innovation in organization design, because it meant that GM had to lean in two directions at once. On the one hand, to succeed with different customers, GM would need more variety in its product line than any manufacturer had ever attempted. On the other, to keep the cars affordable, there would have to be significant sharing of parts and, therefore, coordination of design across the lines.

Sloan solved this conundrum with a new organizational structure, the multidivisional corporation. In his words, it represented a "happy medium . . . between the extremes of pure centralization [Ford's path] and pure decentralization [Durant's]." Separate divisions, each focused on a specific customer, could make better-informed decisions about products and marketing. A strong, professional, central office could coordinate the divisions: assigning each a target market segment, creating appropriate performance measures, and helping them achieve critically important economies of scale in design and purchasing. Without such central coordination, GM's cars would not have been affordable. Sloan's organizational design gave GM focus in marketing and sales, and economies of scale in production and design. In other words, Sloan's structure fit his strategy.

Sloan's innovation—commonplace today—was revolutionary in its time. If the world had wanted nothing but Model Ts (and was willing to want nothing but Model Ts forever) Ford's highly centralized system would have prevailed. It is the one best way to make the Model T. But it is completely focused inward, on manufacturing. Sloan's structure allowed GM to reach out to the market, to be more adaptive, and to grow.

GM was one of a handful of major organizations, including Sears, DuPont, and Standard Oil of New Jersey, to develop the multidivisional structure after World War I. This new corporate form balanced decentralized decision making by people with local knowledge of operations with joint planning, to exploit economies of scale. As a result, it allowed a company to grow by extending its scope into new products and markets without over-burdening a small corps of executives.

Under Sloan's leadership, GM's market share grew to 45 percent by 1940, while Ford's dropped to 16 percent. Henry Ford made fun of GM's organization chart. He said it resembled a tree "heavy with nice round berries, each of which bears the name of a man or an office. . . . It takes about 6 weeks for a message from a man living on a berry at the lower-left hand corner of the chart to reach the president or chairman." This was sour grapes. Sloan's strategy and the organization capable of executing it succeeded brilliantly.

Manage or Buy

Scope refers not only to the breadth of an organization's product line, it also describes the range of activities an organization performs. In 1899, when thirty American car makers produced a total of 2,500 cars, nobody made their own components. They bought them from suppliers. Over time, however, as the industry consolidated and volumes grew, companies like Ford and GM extended the scope of their activities backward into the manufacture of components. In the late 1920s, Ford took vertical integration to an extreme, buying a vast plantation in the Amazon jungle to produce rubber for tires.

Why do companies draw and redraw the lines that define how many of the steps in the value chain they perform themselves? Again, it's a question of matching strategy and structure, of finding the organization best able to deliver a particular configuration of value (the right products at the right price), at a particular moment in time. Consider GM's decision to make its own auto bodies.

In the mid-1920s, as car buyers became more sophisticated, the market began to shift from open roadsters, like the Model T, to cars with closed bodies. Customers wanted comfort year round. In just three years, from 1924 to 1927, closed-body cars went from 43 percent of the market to 85 percent. Auto makers scrambled to keep up with demand and, at the same time, they struggled to keep a lid on the added costs.

GM's solution to both problems—volume and costs—was to ask its major supplier, Fisher Body, to build a plant adjacent to a new GM assembly plant. Putting the two plants side by side would reduce costs—shipping docks at both plants could be eliminated, for example. At the same time, GM would secure a predictable source of car bodies.

Fisher turned GM down. The plant would have been so specialized that it could have served only one customer, GM. Stripped of its bargaining power, Fisher would have been at GM's mercy if the two companies disagreed about price. Economists have a descriptive name for this: they call it the *hold-up* problem. Moreover, Fisher would have become completely dependent on GM's fortunes. It's not surprising, therefore, that Fisher decided against making an investment so lopsided in GM's favor.

Instead, GM bought Fisher outright. In an era when industrial companies were growing ever larger, and when supply markets were far less reliable than they are today, extending the scope of an organization to earlier steps in the value chain (*backward integration*) often made sense for two reasons: first, better coordination lowered costs; second, ownership guaranteed a source of critical raw materials. If your company depends on keeping an expensive assembly line running, you can't afford to run out of parts.

Together, all of the make-or-buy decisions an organization makes determine the scope of its activities. At the heart of the decision is a tradeoff. When you do something yourself, using your own resources and employees, you have more control. This solves one of the fundamental problems of organization: how to *coordinate* the resources and the people you depend on to get the job done. With ownership, you get to set the terms. If GM owns Fisher, for example, GM can dictate Fisher's production schedule, deciding what will be produced and when, in a way that best fits GM's overall needs. Ownership and hierarchical control make it easier to manage a complex system as a system.

However, in solving the *coordination* problem, you run afoul of an equally fundamental problem of organization, the problem of *motivation*. For an organization to perform, every player must be motivated to do his best. The certainty that comes along with ownership tends to dampen that motivation. With ownership you lose the powerful incentive of the marketplace: the nervous edge that keeps arm's-length suppliers (and freelancers) on their toes, the anxiety of competition. As a supplier, a company like Fisher has to worry every day that GM will turn to another supplier. It must innovate and it must keep its costs down. As a wholly owned division of GM, Fisher has a lot more security. It has the equivalent of a guaranteed job for life.

How Toyota Redrew the Lines of Scope and Authority

Toyota will always be remembered for sparking a global revolution in quality. It also deserves to be remembered for setting off a slow chain reaction that has redrawn the lines of authority and ownership in all sorts of industries. Toyota's success raised a question that managers have been wrestling with ever since: What's inside the company's boundaries and what's outside? Toyota showed the world that you could manage a supply chain effectively without owning it and, thus, capture the best of both worlds: the coordination and cooperation that come with *hierarchy* (that is, with ownership), and the motivating power, flexibility, and innovation that come from markets.

At the same time, Toyota's success challenged the way most companies drew the lines of authority within their boundaries. Working effectively across the company's boundaries required new attitudes and practices within them. As a result, long before *empowerment* became an irritating buzzword in the west, Toyota demonstrated the value of a fully engaged workforce. The two changes co-evolved, and both arose less from conscious design than from Toyota's determination to make the best of bad circumstances.

In the 1950s, Toyota was a David among the Goliaths of the auto industry. Postwar Japan was an impoverished nation, starved for resources. A small domestic producer, Toyota lacked both the scale and the capital to compete in the auto industry as the game was then played. Forced by circumstances to make cars differently, Toyota ended up drawing its key organizational lines in ways that challenged the model created in Detroit. When Toyota couldn't afford to build components or own its own parts makers, it had to rely on outside suppliers, not just for raw materials, but also for complex systems, such as brakes. Since it had neither the physical space nor the capital to carry inventory, it had to learn how to operate without it.

This flew in the face of conventional wisdom in two ways. First, it meant sharing information with suppliers, treating them more like partners and less like adversaries. The better your suppliers understand what you're trying to accomplish, the more they can tailor their efforts to fit. Toyota showed that cooperation might better serve everyone's interests. Haggling with suppliers over price was always a win–lose game. Working together to create more value for customers could be a win–win one.

Second, the conventional wisdom in manufacturing was that inventory was a necessary evil. You needed to keep extra parts lying around as a buffer, because you took it for granted that the production process would break down periodically. Rather than risk having to shut down an assembly line because you were short on axles, for example, you kept inventory on hand, just in case.

Unable to afford "just in case," Toyota developed *just in time*. If every step in the production process could be made completely reliable, you could have your suppliers deliver the exact number of components you needed, precisely when you were going to need them. Making the production process reliable meant running factories in new ways. It meant, for example, giving workers the authority to stop the production line when a problem arose. If you keep the line moving, and wait until the end to throw out bad products, not only do you incur more costs but, more important, you miss the opportunity to catch problems at their source. Freeing workers to fix the root causes of poor quality was a major redrawing of organizational lines.

It overturned an enduring legacy of Taylor and Ford, the idea that managers did all the thinking and workers did what they were told. Toyota's employee-led quality circles put problem solving in the hands of shop floor workers. Substituting participation for hierarchy, Toyota developed a host of techniques (collectively known as *Total Quality Management*, or TQM) to improve the quality of the manufacturing process. Product quality also improved dramatically as a result.

Toyota's competitive advantage in cost and quality arose directly from its organizational practices. They presented an alternative to Detroit's command-and-control structures: its shop-floor hierarchy, its functional silos, and its vertical integration. Instead of seeing management as the source of all innovation, Toyota's continuous improvement depended on participation from everyone. Instead of allowing specialized departments to go their own ways, Toyota mobilized crossfunctional teams that could be convened to solve problems. In place of vertical integration, Toyota's much studied and copied supply-chain management demonstrated that cooperation and information sharing across company lines could produce benefits for all parties—for suppliers, for manufacturers, and, most of all, for customers.

Manage or Buy: Outsourcing Is In

The phrase *make or buy* arose in a manufacturing context. For many years, it was applied narrowly to sourcing decisions about the physical inputs—the parts, the components, and raw materials that went into a finished product. Companies typically asked make-buy questions as they were expanding. The question was, Is it time for us to make it ourselves? Today it's more likely that companies are on their way to narrowing their scope, to shedding an activity. So the sourcing question is now reversed, and it is asked about every step of the value-creation process. Can someone else do this better than we can? And if the answer is yes: are they so good that the benefits will offset the transaction costs we will incur? *Transaction costs* occur whenever two parties interact and their work must be coordinated. They include all the costs of finding someone to do the job, contracting with them, communicating with them and so on.

In recent years, transaction costs have dropped sharply. A very simple example will show why. In 1980, when a patient in Los Angeles went to see his doctor, the doctor would examine him, then read her notes into a voice recorder. The next day, a clerical worker on the doctor's payroll would transcribe the notes, then route them back to another clerical worker, who would put them into the patient's file. It might well take a couple of days before the notes were available.

Today, when a doctor in Los Angeles meets with a patient and records her notes, satellite communications whisk the recording to India. Time-zone differences kick in so, while the doctor in California sleeps, her notes are transcribed in Bangalore. When she awakes, she has a hard copy of her patient's records. The job has been done faster—which in medicine can have a big impact on the quality of care—and cheaper. The role of technology is obvious. The fact that there is today an organized market in India for this kind of specialized labor is less obvious, but equally important in its impact on transaction costs.

As a result of these changes in technology and markets, the doctor's office of today can be configured and staffed differently from the office of twenty years ago. The work of processing information—or at least some of it—can now be done outside the doctor's office. This is significant, because health care is an information-intensive industry—30 percent of the costs lie in activities best described as the gathering, processing, and reporting of information. In fact, that description fits much of the work done by modern economies. As technology and globalization have lowered transaction costs, places like India and Ireland are becoming the world's back office. Outsourcing is in.

Ronald Coase won the Nobel Prize in economics in 1991 for his work (dating to the late 1930s) on how transaction costs determine the boundaries of organizations. Coase developed a simple principle to explain organizational size: When it is cheaper to conduct transactions internally (that is, within the bounds of a corporation), organizations grow larger. When it is cheaper to conduct them externally, in the open market, organizations stay small or shrink. As markets become more efficient and competitive, and transaction costs drop, vertical integration loses much of its appeal. If that sounds abstract, picture the woman at her PC in Bangalore.

Today, efficient markets are springing up everywhere, and Coase is much in vogue. In fact, he has become the theoretician of choice for new economy advocates of networking and free agency. (And the phrase *high transaction costs* has entered the vernacular as a kind of shorthand for any interaction with a high hassle factor— a difficult employee who consumes a lot of everyone else's time, for instance.)

The phenomenon that Coase described is timeless, but his ideas seem particularly relevant now, because they explain how new technologies and new markets are enabling us to create organizations whose scope is more narrowly focused on a limited set of activities. The doctor creates value through her medical expertise, not by typing up records. If another organization can do the typing faster, cheaper, and as accurately, then the best system for the patient is one that unbundles doctoring and typing.

Today, management looks at the value chain from the outside

in, from the customer's point of view, and seeks a configuration that delivers the best value overall, regardless of who executes each activity. The assumption that an organization will perform every function from research and product design to manufacturing to marketing, selling, and servicing within its boundaries no longer holds. Organizations come in all sizes and shapes, depending on the value they exist to create.

In industries where value has migrated from physical things to intangibles, manufacturing—once a core activity—may have become peripheral. Many companies no longer make the products that bear their name. Nike is a marketing company, not a maker of sneakers. Disney makes Mickey Mouse, but it lets efficient Asian manufacturers make the tee shirts with Mickey on them. Cisco Systems makes new technology, that is, it generates ideas, even though those ideas are embodied in physical products like routers and switches for the Internet. Highly efficient contract manufacturers, such as Flextronics, Solectron Corp., Jabil Circuit Inc., and SCI Systems Inc., accounted for about 20 percent of the world's electronics output in 2000, and their share has been growing rapidly.

Why do companies like Cisco rely on supply-chain managers who operate factories around the globe? In the 1990s Cisco was constantly introducing new products, then replacing them with newer models within a year. If the company did its own manufacturing, it would incur both the costs of setting up the factories and of repeatedly retooling them. If it guessed wrong about a new product, it would be stuck with an expensive asset it couldn't immediately reuse. Companies like Flextronics, based in San Jose, California, can scale up and down at will not only in a single factory, but in several scattered across the globe. "If one of my customers loses market share," Brad Knight, a Flextronics manager in the boomtown of Guadalajara, Mexico, explained to a *Wall Street Journal* reporter, "I can make it up with the other guy who has taken that market share away."

The basic make-buy logic hasn't changed since Alfred Sloan's day, but the context is vastly different. In a world of more stable product design and unreliable, unresponsive supply markets, it made sense for GM to buy Fisher Body. In an era of idea-led growth, with products changing rapidly and companies like Flextronics able to operate globally, outsourcing may work better. Extranet technology allows Cisco to create tight communications links with its customers, its subcontractors, and its partners, enabling them all to work seamlessly with each other as if they were one vertically integrated enterprise. That's the theory that's being tested. In 2000, about half the customer orders Cisco received via the Web went *directly* to its contractors.

Together, efficient markets and faster, cheaper communication have driven down transaction costs and made virtual integration, of one sort or another, plausible for a growing number of organizations. Anything and everything can be outsourced, from generic administrative functions to the manufacturing process itself. Organizations everywhere are reassessing their boundaries, asking what is best done inside and what outside. They are increasingly focusing on the steps in the value chain that are strategically important, those steps that make the organization unique. Will these new structures be as effective in practice as they look in theory? The jury is still out.

A Warning: Markets Aren't a Panacea

We have come to believe that what Adam Smith referred to as "the invisible hand" of the market is an innately superior way to get just about everything done. And even though we're unlikely to see an economy consisting only of electronically connected freelancers, there isn't an organization around whose way of doing things isn't called into question by the ascendancy of markets. Nevertheless, markets aren't a panacea. They aren't always better than the visible hand of management. Consider this cau-

tionary tale about the National Basketball Association, an affilia-
tion of independently owned teams that lost 20 percent of its
prime-time television audience in 1999.

For many basketball fans, the reason to watch a game isn't the
team but a single outstanding player, like a Michael Jordan or a
Larry Bird. In the past, stars such as these joined the pros after
playing four years of college ball. By the time they'd reached the
NBA, they'd already developed a large following among the fans.
This system has broken down under the combined weight of free
agency and internal competition among the teams. Lured by the
big checks that owners will write for talent, kids are dropping out
of school so fast that no one knows or cares who they are. As a
result, the owners are not only paying more for the players but
also spending more to market them—not very successfully—to
the fans.

At one level, this is simply another example of the market
dynamics we've looked at before. The players' talent is the scarce
resource and, since free agency gives them more power vis-à-vis
the owners, they are getting a bigger slice of the pie. But this story
is far more interesting as a failure of markets to accomplish the
larger purposes that managed organizations are capable of. Both
the teams and the kids are acting in their own self-interest. And
self-interest is the invisible hand that supposedly directs results to
the best outcome overall. What the defection of the fans tells us,
though, is that the NBA's product is less valuable overall. At least
in the years surrounding 2000, the pie itself was getting smaller.
The value of the whole system for customers is shrinking because
no one is in charge. No one is managing the whole to maximize
value creation.

What's unfolding in the NBA is an athletic version of the
tragedy of the commons: Everyone is acting in his own self-
interest, no one has any incentive to think about the health of the
game overall, and the NBA lacks the centralized power to force

everyone to restrain themselves for the good of all. That's what managed organizations can do, and markets can't. In this instance, a little hierarchical authority might be a useful thing.

Global Markets, Global Scale

Even as the spread of markets is encouraging organizations to break apart into more focused pieces, in most industries, the overall trend is toward ever-bigger giants. If you want to play in the auto industry, you have to be vastly bigger than you needed to be in Henry Ford's day, or even twenty-five years ago. The same is true in pharmaceuticals, in telecommunications, in oil, in financial services. Each industry has its own scale requirements, and those change as the competitive arena changes, but many industries today are moving in the direction of bigger.

If we look at how organizations grew big in the first place, it will be clear why scale has been changing once again. Before the nineteenth century, most markets were local. Before the steamship, the railroad, and the telegraph, it was too expensive and too unreliable to try to do business outside the narrowest of geographic boundaries. Small enterprises matched the needs of small local markets. With the emergence of national markets and the spread of new industrial technologies, enterprises had to become larger in order to be efficient.

Today, analogous forces are once again transforming the context in which organizations operate. The ability to exchange information and goods faster and more cheaply, coupled with political changes that favor world trade, means that scale is becoming global in many industries. Changes in the sources of value creation are also important. In Henry Ford's day, capital was the scarce resource that organizations were designed to use efficiently, as his assembly line did. In today's knowledge-based economy, talent and ideas play a bigger role in determining an industry's scale requirements.

Conventional wisdom in the auto industry, for example, is that a company needs to sell four million cars per year just to stay in the game. That's why the industry has been consolidating, with once independent makers merging and acquiring each other. Why have the stakes risen so dramatically? Today, even the automobile industry is driven more by the economics of ideas than the economics of physical production. Car companies need to be bigger than ever, because they face huge costs in brand marketing, in entering difficult new markets, and in developing new technology.

Honda is one of the few smaller auto companies staying independent—at least at the time of this writing. And Honda adds an interesting twist to this discussion of where to draw an organization's lines. Among the biggest R&D costs facing automakers are those required to develop cleaner engines. It can cost $500 million to develop a new conventional engine, and far more for a gas-electric hybrid or fuel-cell-powered motor. The need to spread these costs over high sales volume creates huge pressure to expand. (The same logic applies to the cost of developing new drugs or discovering new oil fields.)

Producing two million cars per year, Honda is a small car company, but it's a giant in engines, which represent 10 percent of the cost of a car. Counting the motors it makes for lawnmowers and motorcycles, Honda is the world's biggest maker of internal-combustion engines—manufacturing about 10 million per year. Because Honda can share the cost of engine development across its product lines, this scope advantage may compensate for its overall lack of scale.

Moreover, Honda's focus on engines might result in different cars that customers will choose over alternatives. That is, Honda's organization may reinforce its strategy. Most auto makers who sponsor F1 racing subcontract engine design to others. Not Honda. It takes what it learns from its racing program and puts it into the engines for the Accord and other vehicles. Honda's

Insight was the first mass-market car in the United States with a hybrid gas and electric engine. Moreover, just as Intel has branded the chips that drive computers, Honda is positioning itself to become a brand-name supplier of engines to other car makers. (In 1999, for example, Honda struck a deal to supply GM with one hundred thousand advanced V-6 engines a year.) Honda president Hiroyuki Yoshino vows to remain independent. "We believe success has little to do with size," he told the *Wall Street Journal*. But if Honda succeeds, it will be because it has organized to be first and foremost in engines.

Organizing to Tackle Society's Biggest Problems

All organizations, nonprofits included, must match their design to the missions they undertake. In the social sector, however, scale is often a poignant problem. Many nonprofits tackle huge problems (hunger, poverty, disease) with disproportionately limited resources. When Microsoft founder Bill Gates burst onto the philanthropic scene in the 1990s, the expected size of his giving was cause for new hope. "Gates money," as it is called in the nonprofit world, has the potential to change the landscape, making it plausible for the first time for many organizations to match the scale of their efforts to the problems they're trying to address. At the same time, other major foundations—seeking to apply management principles more systematically—are rethinking their strategies, deliberately cutting back their scope to focus more narrowly on missions where they can expect to achieve greater impact.

India's Aravind Eye Hospital is a mission-driven organization whose success illustrates the kind of impact that can be achieved when the lines of organization are drawn in support of strategy. Aravind has made smart choices about scale, scope, and structure since its founding in 1976 by a retired eye surgeon, Dr. Govindappa Venkataswamy. He started small, with a twenty-bed private, nonprofit hospital. Within 25 years, Aravind has become the largest provider of eye surgery in the world, performing 180,000 cataract operations a year, 70 percent of them for free.

Dr. V's vision and his methods owe a lot to Henry Ford. (Dr. V himself credits McDonald's as his inspiration; the principles are the same.) In India, millions of people suffer from blindness due to cataracts. Most can be cured with a simple operation. The management challenge is to make that operation affordable. Dr. V's dream, in a sense, was to build an eye hospital for the multitudes.

Cataract surgery is Dr. V's Model T. Focusing on this one "product," Aravind has designed an extraordinarily efficient, high-volume, assembly-line process to produce it. Every step has been standardized, from patient screening and registration to the surgery itself. The operating theater is designed to maximize the productivity of the surgeons. While a surgeon operates on one patient, the next is being prepped on a second table. When the first operation ends, the surgeon can turn immediately to start the next one. And so on, back and forth.

And, yes, the surgeons have given up some autonomy to follow, step by step, a standardized operating procedure. We may dismiss Henry Ford's command and control style as a throwback to the industrial age, but standardization as a design principle is alive and well, and still works miracles of productivity. According to one recent report, it costs Aravind about $10 to perform a cataract operation that costs a typical United States hospital $1,650.

A significant cost of cataract surgery is the intraocular lens that's inserted to replace the patient's clouded lens. By the early 1990s, Aravind was buying lenses in such high volumes that it felt it could lower its costs by backward integrating into lens production. It created Aurolab, which today produces lenses on a global scale, manufacturing seven hundred thousand per year. Aravind meets its own needs and sells the rest to other providers.

Once Aravind got off the ground, Dr. V subdivided its operations into two separate facilities, located close to each other. One is for patients who pay, the other for those treated free. The amenities are nicer at the paying hospital than they are at the free hospital, but both share the same staff of doctors and nurses, so all patients get the same high-quality medical care. Aravind's strategy, then, borrows from Sloan's. It is eye care for different purses and purposes. Keeping the two units separate but adjacent lets Aravind attract paying customers without compromising on the quality of care for the indigent.

The paying patients are critical to Aravind's success, making the organization self-sustaining. Those patients are drawn to Aravind by its reputation for world-class eye care. Here too, organization supports strategy. Aravind has forged research and training collaborations with premier teaching hospitals in the United States. Aravind may be low cost overall, but it stays at the leading edge of its field, and that is its appeal to paying customers. It is also part of Aravind's appeal to its doctors. They work longer hours, for less money, in exchange for the psychic rewards that come in part from professional pride, in part from the organization's social mission. Thus, Aravind has drawn the lines on incentives in ways that reinforce its strategy.

Aravind and the other organizations described in this chapter illustrate a fundamental point: Despite all the claims by management writers to the contrary, there is no one best way to organize. Scale, scope, and structure are enormously contingent on what you're trying to do. One big problem with organizational fashions is that everyone likes to try them on. Companies outsource or acquire because everyone is doing it. Or, they shy away from top-down directives where they're needed because the appearance of authority is politically incorrect.

Were we able to follow these organizations in greater detail and over time, they would also illustrate another fundamental point.

Designing an organization is an exercise in frustration. Time and events will inevitably overtake the best-laid plan: One way or another, you'll outgrow the design. You'll erase here, and redraw there, and, because the whole is a complex system, a change in one place will show up as an unintended consequence someplace else. Organizations are always slipping out of alignment.

Designing an organization is also frustrating, because most of the important decisions are at best tradeoffs you'd rather not have to make—you'll gain coordination here, but lose it there. You choose the best option, knowing that what you've *not* chosen can come back to haunt you. Treat the latest approach as a panacea, as the relentlessly upbeat literature on the subject has a tendency to do, and you will surely be disappointed. Understand the tradeoffs that have been made well enough to compensate for them, and everyone will perform better, whether it comes to drawing new lines or living within the existing ones.

Part II

Execution: Making It Happen

"In the end, a vision without the ability to execute is probably a hallucination."

—Stephen M. Case,
Chairman, AOL Time Warner

Chapter 5

Facing Reality: Which Numbers Matter and Why

Not everything that can be counted counts, and not everything that counts can be counted.

—Albert Einstein

The concepts explored in part I are critical to creating good plans. Now we turn to the subject of execution, translating plans into performance. This brief chapter prepares the way for those to follow by explaining why numbers are critical to execution, and by describing the basic numeracy everyone in an organization needs. Like any profession, management has developed its own specialized vocabulary, much of it quantitative. This numeric world can be dauntingly forbidding to outsiders. There's no reason that it should be. The numbers that matter are the ones that help you to face reality, and to do something about it. Consider:

On July 25, 2000, an Air France Concorde jet exploded shortly after takeoff, when a tire blew out and hit the plane's fuel tank. The crash left 113 people dead. These were the first Concorde fatalities in the supersonic jet's thirty-one-year history. Within days, the Concorde, pride of the European consortium Airbus, was grounded indefinitely.

Why was the world's fastest passenger jet suddenly taken out of service? There had been only three disintegrating tire incidents over thirty-one years, and none had caused a plane to crash before. How bad a safety record is that?

In a word, unacceptable—but that's clear only when you compare the number of incidents to the total number of times the Concorde has flown. Because there were so few Concorde jets in service and just a few flights per day, the failure rate was extraordinarily high. If that rate were applied to the fleet of U.S. airlines in service, it would produce one serious tire explosion—sending flying debris into the fuselage or engine—per day. One per day! That's why the Concorde was grounded. And it's why management requires the discipline of quantification. Simple numbers help us to face reality and to make sense of events in ways that our intuition alone cannot do.

Numbers are essential to organizational performance. But basic managerial numeracy isn't rocket science, and there's no need for anyone to be intimidated by the math. For at least the past couple of decades, first year M.B.A. students at the Harvard Business School have been assigned a short note with the title, "How to Avoid Getting Lost in the Numbers." Given the stereotype of the Harvard M.B.A., most people might be surprised to discover that "the numbers" have a lot more to do with common sense than math beyond the high school level. The real skill is making sense of the numbers, not crunching them. Sometimes, however, you need to understand how the number was crunched to see its significance.

Doing the numbers begins with the simple act of measurement. If you want to know, objectively, how much you weigh you have to get on the scale. The same is true of organizations. Taking that first step requires discipline. It's not something most of us do naturally or even willingly. It's not unusual to be overconfident and insecure at the same time, to think you're doing better than you are, on the one hand, and to be anxious about what the numbers will reveal, on the other. It takes discipline to face reality, and to capture that reality objectively and unambiguously, so that everyone in the organization works from a common fact base, and people aren't left to come up with their own interpretations. "When everybody gets the same facts," as Jack Welch put it, "they'll generally come to the same conclusion."

Measurement is necessary but not sufficient, however. Ultimately, the numbers that truly matter are the ones that tell a story about how the organization is doing. To turn a piece of data into a meaningful story you must put it in context. Go back to the scale for a moment. If we learn that Tyler weighs 145 pounds we know something objective, but it isn't, to use the managerial term, "actionable." If we learn next that Tyler is a six-foot-tall man the data begins to tell one story. If Tyler is a five-foot-tall woman, it's quite another story. Now add one more piece of context. Suppose we learn that three months ago, Tyler weighed two hundred pounds. This gives us not just a story, but a call for urgent intervention, at least in the man's case. For the woman, we'd need to ask for more information to know whether the news was good or bad.

Most of the numbers that seem like so much inside baseball to non-managers are simple ratios that, like the Concorde's failure rate, compare one dimension of performance to some clear reference point. Often expressed as percentages or fractions, these ratios are, in essence, batting averages. They keep track of your successes compared to the number of times you step up to the plate. Consider *six sigma,* a quality measure that has been all the rage for the past decade (and will continue to be so for at least the next decade, if not longer). While it is a religion at companies like Motorola and GE, and Greek to most people, six sigma is basically just a batting average that tells you what percentage of your efforts are error-free.

Sigma is the symbol used by statisticians to represent a standard deviation. One sigma means 68 percent of your output is acceptable. Three sigma means that you've succeeded 97 percent of the time. At six sigma, 99.999997 percent of the products you've made are acceptable. In other words, there are only 3.4 defects per million operations. In the late 1990s, many companies were operating at around 3.5 sigma, or 35,000 defects per million. This was true whether you were looking at manufacturing operations or the writing up of restaurant bills, payroll processing, and doctor's prescriptions. Airlines were in the 35,000 to 50,000 range with their baggage-handling operations. While we might grumble about that, it still meant that most of us got our bags at the end of a flight. When it comes to safety, however, the airlines *exceed* six sigma, with less than one failure for every two million operations. And that's as it should be—and as the Concorde wasn't.

Which ratios you look at depends on who you are and why you want to know. An investor thinking about whether to loan money to a company is especially interested in measures that capture its ability to pay him back. Someone managing a call center will be more interested in measures that help her reduce the amount of time that customers sit waiting on hold.

Numbers that reveal trends are related to ratios. A time series follows a measure over time, a company's revenues or costs over the past five years, for instance. (Growth rates are simply ratios that compare today to yesterday.) Like ratios, *trend data* create meaning by putting numbers into context. Consider this example from Apple Computer.

Despite its small share of the total market for personal computers, Apple has long been a leader in sales to schools and universities. When CEO Steve Jobs learned that Apple's share of computer sales to schools was 12.5 percent in 1999, he was dismayed, but unless you're an industry analyst who knows the numbers cold, you won't appreciate just how dismayed he was. That's because, in 1998, Apple was the segment leader with a market share of 14.6 percent. And, while Apple slipped to the number two spot in 1999, Dell grew and took the lead with 15.1 percent. Alone each number is meaningless. Together they spell trouble. If you're Steve Jobs, you see a trend that you'd better figure out how to reverse. This isn't number crunching, it's sense making.

It is always helpful to remember that numbers don't have a life of their own. They summarize the behavior of actual people doing real things. Think, for example, about what happens when a new technology hits the market, whether it's a DVD player or a cell phone or e-mail. First, a few people try it. Then, the new thing gets better and cheaper. People who tried it early on, and were willing to pay a lot for it, assure the rest of us that it really works. So, more people try it. Soon, it really takes off, and everyone has to have it. Then, after everyone has it, the growth slows way down. That's a pattern of consumer behavior almost all of us have participated in and anyone can understand. It applied to George Eastman's cameras 100 years ago, and it's true of cell phones today.

Most people would have more trouble grasping the concept, however, were it described not as human behavior, but as the slope of an *S-curve* (or penetration curve). The mathphobes in the audience would probably have felt that they were now in over their heads, that they had entered a realm that was too hard. True number crunchers, on the other hand, might be at ease with the sophisticated math behind an S-curve, but might not connect the mathematical equation describing the curve with the human behavior that produced it. Between these extremes, good managers use numbers to create a common middle ground of purposeful action. What the numbers do is allow you to see the larger patterns unfolding so that you can take appropriate action. If you're in the cell-phone business, for instance, knowing where you are on the penetration curve will make a big difference in how you think about your marketing efforts or your supply chain.

There's nothing magic in the math behind familiar patterns, as long as you don't lose sight of the underlying human behavior that creates the pattern in the first place. It's easy to focus so intently on the numbers alone, that you forget that they reflect what people are doing. At the same time, without the numbers, you wouldn't see larger patterns unfolding.

In the end, it's not the math that's hard—at least for most of the work general managers do. Anyone can be taught *how* to calculate a basic ratio in a matter of minutes, whether it's an error rate or return on investment. They can be taught *why* to do those calculations in a matter of hours. Why is the debt ratio so important, for example? Because it says something about your ability to pay off your obligations to creditors: The more debt you carry (in relation to your ability to generate cash), the more risk for the lender that you will run short of cash.

What is harder and takes longer is developing judgment about *what the number means*. Interpreting a number requires experience that allows you to develop a set of norms or expectations about what the number should look like. Experience gives you some feeling for relative and relevant magnitudes—just as everyone knows how to react to the figures of Tyler's weight and weight loss. Likewise, experience teaches you to respond to one number by seeking others that will help to flesh out the story.

Numbers No Organization Can Live Without

In chapter 2, we described business models as stories, and focused on narrative logic as the test of a good model. Does the story make sense? Is it based on a sound understanding of who the principal characters are and how those characters are likely to behave? Numbers take you an important step further. If the narrative makes sense, the numbers will add up.

If your story about who your customers are and what they value makes sense, it will show up in the top line, in your revenues. If your story about how you will create value makes sense, that will show up in your costs. If your story about how you are different from other alternatives makes sense, it will show up in your profits and in your ability to generate cash. Revenues, costs, profits, and cash flow are the numbers no organization can live without.

The real story behind many of the failed ventures in the first wave of e-commerce is that this basic business math was missing. The grocery business, for example, has very thin margins to begin with. So, if customers won't pay more for their purchases, and you're adding costs in service and delivery without eliminating them anywhere else, there's no way you can make the math work, as companies like Webvan discovered.

Both a firm grasp of the basics and the ability to make sense of numbers have become more critical than ever, because technology is continually increasing the amount of information at our disposal. With the advent of zip codes, area codes, credit card numbers, cookies, and so on, data collection and data mining have become professions. Computing power makes it feasible to match up numbers from different data sets. For example, a drug company today can learn precisely which doctors, by name, are prescribing which drugs.

Not only do managers have more data at their disposal than ever before, they have it faster, in so-called *real time*. Instead of getting information after the fact—often long after—you get it in time to intervene. You get to fix things on the fly. Real-time data about airline bookings, for example, allows sophisticated software to adjust fares just in time to fill seats that otherwise would have flown empty. *Load management*, as it is called, can make the difference between whether an airline makes money or loses it.

With so much data coming at you so fast, it is more important than ever not to get lost in the numbers, to keep a clear head about what you're trying to do, and which numbers can help you find your way or stay on course. Without measurement, progress would be impossible. That said, however, managers have also been prone to periodic bouts of hubris, becoming so enamored of the quantitative tools they devise that they forget that tools are only aids to judgment. Even the best stopwatch won't tell you what time it is, let alone how you should be spending your time.

Consider the legacy of the Whiz Kids. During World War II, a special unit trained at the Harvard Business School in the latest quantitative approaches to decision making helped the United States achieve extraordinary performance in manufacturing and logistics. Before the war, the Army Air Corps (precursor of the U.S. Air Force) had only about four hundred planes. By war's end, the force commanded 230,000 planes, and the spare parts it took to keep them flying. Moving men and materials on that scale was an enormous feat. After working such miracles through numbers, the so-called Whiz Kids went on to leave their mark on corporate America.

Robert McNamara, a leading figure of this generation, brought a management-by-the-numbers approach to the Ford Motor Company, when he was hired by Henry Ford II, Henry's grandson, in 1949. Ford was in bad shape, desperately in need of financial controls, and McNamara was given license to build a large and powerful staff. They were soon dubbed *bean counters* by the product men who resented both their rapid rise to power and their ignorance of cars. The derisive term has become a permanent part of our language, referring to those who use numbers without understanding their significance.

In the 1970s, the Ford Pinto taught the nation the basics of cost-benefit analysis. The car had a design flaw in the gas tank that caused at least fifty-nine deaths. Rubber liners would have fixed the problem at a cost of $137 million. But careful calculations of the benefits—all the costs associated with those burned and killed down to the flowers at the funeral—only added up to $49.5 million. Cost-benefit analysis said it just didn't pay to redesign the Pinto.

The lesson at the time seemed pretty clear, and many baby boomers grew up suspicious about management and its methods. They believed, to paraphrase Oscar Wilde, that managers were people who knew the price of everything and the value of nothing. That suspicion still lingers, especially in the nonprofit sector. But the fact is that the same set of tools that created the Ford Pinto defeated fascism in World War II. Tools are just that.

This is a lesson that needs to be relearned periodically. Dazzled as we are by advances in computing power, it's tempting to think that, because you can assemble and manipulate the numbers as never before, you can also control events. Whether finance will ever be a true science, as the finance professors would like to believe, it is certainly evolving in that direction. However, the spectacular failure in 1998 of Long Term Capital Management should serve as a warning.

LTCM was a hedge fund, run by a team of finance whizzes, including a couple of Nobel laureates. They applied their theories about mastering risk to the realities of global capital markets with disastrous results. They used a technique called "dynamic hedging," which involves offsetting risks by placing bets in opposite directions. The technique is a form of insurance that gives investors the confidence to take on investments with which they wouldn't otherwise be comfortable. LTCM's dynamic hedging was based on the historical relationships between markets around the world, the fact that one market tended to go up when another went down. In the face of the Asian panic, then crises in Russia, LTCM kept betting that those historic relationships would reassert themselves. They didn't, at least not fast enough to prevent LTCM's collapse from shaking global capital markets.

It is a useful reminder of a critical point: Business and markets are about people and their complex behavior. Thanks to the coevolution of the discipline of finance and the capabilities of computing devices, we have better tools for understanding and managing risk. But the tools are only aids to judgment. Simple numbers properly used help organizations understand what's going on, to take their bearings so that they can get where they're going. They discipline us to face reality. The mathematician John Allen Paulos put it nicely: "Describing the world may be thought of as an Olympic contest between simplifiers—scientists in general, statisticians in particular—and complicators—humanists in general, storytellers in particular. It is a contest both should win."

Chapter 6

The *Real* Bottom Line: Mission and Measures

The bottom line is down where it belongs—at the bottom. Far above it in importance are the infinite number of events that produce the profit or loss.

—Paul Hawken,
founder, Smith and Hawken

One of the most powerful management disciplines, the one that more than any other keeps people focused and pulling in the same direction, is to make an organization's purposes tangible. Managers do this by translating the organization's mission—what it, particularly, exists to do—into a set of goals and performance measures that make success concrete for everyone. This is the *real* bottom line for every organization—whether it's a business or a school or a hospital. Its executives must answer the question, "Given our mission, how is our performance going to be defined?" This chapter will explain how an organization's purpose determines what results are meaningful and what measures are appropriate. Figuring that out is a lot harder to do than it sounds.

In fact, performance measures are rarely obvious Milton Hershey, the chocolate tycoon, died in 1945. An orphan himself, Hershey founded a school in 1909 for the "maintenance, support, and education" of poor orphan boys. By the late 1990s, the Milton Hershey School faced a peculiar problem. The bull market of the 1990s had propelled the school's endowment into the stratosphere. In 1998, it stood at $5 billion, bigger than Stanford's, MIT's, and that of all but five of the richest U.S. universities. The problem: The school couldn't spend money fast enough to satisfy the legal requirement of the Hershey trust.

What does this have to do with management and the performance of organizations? The Hershey School's one thousand or so well-dressed students enjoy a beautiful, sprawling campus equipped with the finest facilities money can buy. At sixty thousand dollars per pupil per year, it's hard to imagine how the school could spend more on them. Warring factions have lined up with competing ideas as to how to spend the Hershey money. In essence, they are arguing over how the Hershey trust should translate its mission into concrete measures of performance that will signal to everyone the organization's priorities.

Some think that a research institute to study learning and development would best execute the trust's mission. They would measure performance by the new knowledge they create. Others are horrified at the idea of a think tank, arguing that the primary beneficiaries will be contractors and consultants, not needy kids. But even narrowing the focus to how best to benefit needy kids leads to competing views of performance. Some advocate using the money to increase the school's enrollments. For them, the number of students who are helped is the best measure. Others say, don't expand the size of the school, extend the scope of its aid by putting more money into college scholarships for the kids once they leave the Hershey School. For them, performance isn't how many kids are helped but how much help each kid gets.

Because the money comes from a trust, a probate court will have to determine what Hershey intended. But the story illustrates one of the most fundamental managerial challenges of all: translating mission into action and into performance. Here, the courts will decide. In most cases, that's management's job (or the board's). The reason this is a challenge is that there's almost never one right answer, and this is true whether the organization is a business or a social enterprise. Yet, without a clear answer, individuals in an organization will provide their own—and operate under their own assumptions and interpretations.

One of the stereotypes of modern management is that it is focused—to the exclusion of just about everything else—on the bottom line. It is absolutely true that one of the defining characteristics of good managers is that they consistently "meet their numbers." Nevertheless, the stereotype of the manager obsessed with the bottom line blurs a crucially important distinction between an organization's purpose—what it uniquely exists to do—and the end results of achieving that purpose. Profits are a result, not a purpose. As David Packard, the legendary cofounder of Hewlett-Packard put it, "Profit is not the proper end and aim of management—it is what makes all of the proper ends and aims possible."

Now that we have become a nation of shareholders and investors, we are more likely than ever to think that the purpose of a business is to generate profits. (The meteoric rise and fall of the profitless dot.coms was the exception that ultimately proved the rule.) This interpretation is regularly reinforced by the media and by many managers themselves. But the real purpose of any business is to create value for its customers and to generate profits as a result.

While the distinction between purpose and results may sound like hair splitting, it's not. It goes to the heart of how managers get organizations to perform. Performance is never a matter of simply issuing an edict or an e-mail to everyone directing them to earn $1.23 per share. Organizations are intentional creations: They are where we come together to accomplish something that none of us could achieve alone. But there is nothing automatic about this coming-together process. By chance, we might stumble upon a viable purpose and find ways to cooperate, contribute, and organize ourselves: but it's not likely. "The only things that evolve by themselves in an organization," Peter Drucker once observed wryly, "are disorder, friction, and malperformance." Despite all the attention given to the bottom line, there is no formula, no one magic number, that captures the purpose of every organization. If there were, management would be far less challenging and interesting than it is.

From the Model T to the Mars Mission: Good and Bad Measures

When Henry Ford started his company in 1903, his partners wanted him to make high-priced cars with high margins. Ford's co-owners were typical of early investors in the auto industry in thinking that profit per car was the best measure of performance. Ford balked at this. His purpose, his overriding goal was to "build a car for the great multitude," to democratize the auto. Ford wanted to create a car so affordable that it would displace the horse; he wanted cars to be so common that one day, hard as it must have been to imagine at the time, they would be "taken for granted."

By 1907, Ford had bought up enough shares in the company to assume a majority position. He used his new control to shift the company's direction. For him, the measure of success was the number of cars sold. Selling a lot of cars, at a "reasonably small profit" would allow him to satisfy his two chief aims in life: more people could buy and enjoy cars, and more men could have good jobs at good wages. Ford created the "people's car" by reducing prices by 58 percent from 1908 to 1916, at a time when he had more orders than he could fill, and could easily have raised them. Ford's shareholders responded by slapping him with a suit against the practice. At the same time, he instituted the five-dollar day for workers, double the industry's standard wage. The *Wall Street Journal* condemned Ford for injecting "spiritual principles into a field where they don't belong."

With 20-20 hindsight (and a better understanding of value creation), we can understand why Ford's measure was the right one, the one that fit his purpose, his business model and, for a time, the competitive realities of the nascent auto industry. It led Ford to make the right pricing decision, that is, the one that supported his overriding purpose. At a time when turnover in the industry was astronomically high and, therefore, a real threat to Ford's ability to churn out its unprecedented volume of cars, it also led him to make the right decision about wages, which was the key people decision of the day. (The five-dollar-per-day wage also turned workers into customers who could afford cars.)

With the same kind of 20-20 hindsight, we can also understand why the U.S. space agency, NASA, chose the wrong measures for its Mars program in the late 1990s. Under the pressure imposed by shrinking federal budgets, NASA was forced to change its approach to space exploration. Abandoning huge, billion-dollar, decade-long missions, it settled on a strategy that called for many smaller projects, each lasting two to three years, and costing a few hundred million dollars. NASA's administrator, Daniel S. Goldin, defined performance for the organization as doing more with less.

The new approach was dubbed "faster, cheaper, better," and this became the definition of success for everyone at NASA. In the wake of the December 3, 1999 crash of the *Mars Polar Lander*, however, just months after the loss of its companion craft, the *Mars Climate Orbiter*, investigators suggested that NASA's "faster, cheaper, better" approach to space missions might have gone too far. Faulty switches on the landing legs cut the craft's engines off too soon, causing the $165 million *Lander* to crash into the surface of Mars. Had NASA not been cutting corners on its premission testing, this sort of problem would have surfaced and could easily have been corrected by a programming change in the spacecraft's computer. The $125 million *Orbiter* was similarly lost through the kind of minor oversight that happens when you're in a rush: a programming glitch in the navigation system that failed to convert English measurements to metric. Apparently, cost cutting and tight schedules had been emphasized at the expense of quality.

Easy as it is to criticize NASA's management, it's more important to draw the right lesson from the story, which is not simply that they chose the wrong definition of success, but how hard it is to get the definition right. NASA's budget constraints were very real. The measures they chose did their job, in part, by communicating that reality to everyone involved in the Mars program. It was the countervailing measures NASA management failed to use that undermined the Mars mission.

For most organizations, performance is multifaceted; it comes from striking the right balance. No one measure can capture 100 percent of what an organization needs to do to perform. And, like medicines, all measures have side effects, some of which can be dangerous to an organization's health. In short, you can't manage without measures, but neither can you apply them without thinking long and hard about how well they fit what you have to do.

In Search of the Universal Measure

It may be the oldest saw in the book, yet it remains absolutely true: What gets measured gets managed. Without measurement, there is no performance. Measures help organizations map their course as they venture into uncharted territory. Good measures help you to find your way; they signal when you need to make midcourse adjustments in direction or in speed. They also serve as a kind of beacon for everyone in the organization, providing a common goal and a common language for talking about it.

For this reason, efforts to find the right way to keep score have been management's version of the search for the holy grail. Periodically, there is a new claimant for the One Right Measure that will tell managers everything they need to know to run a business. EVA, short for economic value added, is the most recent candidate and a current buzzword. Return on investment (ROI) has been one of the most persistent.

Would that it were so simple. It is as if one measure—your blood pressure, say, or your cholesterol level—could tell you and everyone else who has an interest in your health (your family, your employer, your insurance company) everything they need to know. This is why the holy-grail analogy is apt: It's a noble quest, but inherently impossible.

Consider the bottom line, certainly one of the acid tests of value creation. It's not a perfect measure, but it is the first place to look for some objective gauge of how you're doing. You know you've created value for customers if they are willing to foot the bill, and the bill includes the cost of all the resources that go into serving them. Profit is one of those costs. A healthy bottom line tells you that the customer values what you do. It probably also tells you that you're doing a reasonable job of keeping your costs in line, because failure to do so will show up in slimmer profit margins. If you do a poor job of creating value for customers, it will show up in lost sales or in downward pressure on your prices. So, the bottom line is a good indicator of how well you're doing, at least for the short term.

The bottom line doesn't tell you everything, however. As a longer-term indicator, it's problematic. It says nothing about sustainability. It says nothing about whether you've fattened profits by gouging your customers on price, for example. Or whether you decided to cut spending this quarter on new product development or customer service. Any of those actions will boost the bottom line today, but leave you with a sick business tomorrow.

Developing the measures that make organizations manageable has been an evolutionary process. As new management challenges arose, new metrics were created to address them. The industrial revolution, for example, gave birth to a host of basic efficiency measures. These were derived by counting inputs and outputs to come up with the cost per pound of producing textiles, for instance, or the cost per mile of track, a measure used to compare the performance of the men managing a railroad.

As enterprises grew larger and more complex, owners had to hire supervisors and middle managers: they then needed information and reporting systems to guide, control, and evaluate the managers. When Alfred Sloan was turning General Motors into a working whole, he realized that in order to replace "management by crony, with the divisions operating on a horse-trading basis," he needed measures that could compare performance across different kinds of activities. Comparing the efficiency of an assembly plant to the efficiency of a factory that makes spark plugs would be like comparing apples to oranges.

Financial measures provided the common denominator that made comparison possible. Thus, Sloan's head of finance, Donaldson Brown, developed a way to measure the rate of return on the money invested in each business. Financial efficiency, how productively each of those operations uses capital, was, and is, the point of ROI, the best known and most widely used of all the financial measures of performance. It was one of the metrics that gave managers control over what was to become the world's largest corporation.

As is often the case, however, the success of ROI was also its undoing. By the 1960s and 1970s, financial measures, especially ROI, so dominated management thinking that many managers focused more on the numbers than on the underlying realities those numbers reflected. The wakeup call came in the form of an influential *Harvard Business Review* article by Robert Hayes and William Abernathy, published in 1980 with the title "Managing our Way to Economic Decline." It argued persuasively that overreliance on short-term financial measures like ROI could lead to the slow death of investment in the innovation that is the lifeblood of most organizations.

The value revolution of the past two decades addressed this

problem. Now, managers use an arsenal of measures aimed not just at toting up, after the fact, how well an organization has done. Instead, a host of finer-grained measures—tailored to the specific organization—are used proactively to improve performance. Operating measures and financial measures tell managers how well they're using resources, people, physical facilities, and capital. Measures of employee turnover are an important barometer of the climate inside an organization. Measures of external performance, such as customer satisfaction and loyalty (retention rates, for example, and repeat sales) and market share give managers a handle on how well the organization is doing at creating value for customers, as well as a way of keeping score against rivals.

As imperfect as any one measure might be, it's impossible to work systematically on performance without them. Good managers know they can't live without performance measures, but neither can they live by them without respecting their limitations, as NASA's failures illustrate. They use measures flexibly, as tools, almost always in combination, and they create new ones as they confront new performance challenges.

Mission Critical

Listen to people in an organization long enough and you will surely hear some acronym—ROI, SVA, ROIC, EVA, EBIT—that will tell you a lot about the organization's priorities. Thoughtless managers use standard measures as if they had a validity of their own. In well-managed organizations, the critical measures are carefully selected from the larger arsenal for their fit with the mission and strategy of the enterprise and the current realities of its situation.

"Turnarounds"—companies in deep trouble—face a very stark current reality. Figure out quickly where you are, or you will crash and burn. Managers with a track record of bringing failing companies back to life are called "turnaround artists," but this is a case where discipline matters more than any art. Turnarounds make it easy to see the power of translating what the organization needs to do into simple measures of performance that everyone can understand.

To illustrate, consider this vignette from the turnaround of Continental Airlines, described by its president, Greg Brenneman. The year was 1994, and 18 percent of Continental's flights were cash negative. Aware that the fastest way to make money is to stop losing it, Brenneman "sat the scheduling team down and started asking questions."

> "Why are we going from Greensboro to Greenville six times a day when both customers who want to fly that route are on the first flight?"
>
> "It's strategic," someone told me.
>
> "When did it last make money?"
>
> "It never did," was the reply.
>
> "How strategic can that be?"
>
> There was silence. I asked,
>
> "Does someone's boyfriend or girlfriend live there? Why don't we just charter you a Lear jet? It would be cheaper."

The result: This route and other cash drainers were cut.

The turnaround strategy for Continental, says Brenneman, "wasn't complex; it was pure common sense." Stop flying 120-seat planes with thirty passengers. Get people and their bags to their destinations on time. Feed them when they're hungry. Create an atmosphere in which people like coming to work. What measures did they track to see whether they were translating these goals into performance? The monthly load factor, revenue per available seat mile, monthly on-time performance, mishandled bags, turnover, and sick leave. As Brenneman says, "The foundation of any successfully run business is a strategy everyone understands coupled with a few key measures that are routinely tracked."

Matching Measures to Mission

Continental's situation was urgent; without the right measures and actions the company would have failed, and failed quickly. Facing extinction, as Continental did, can bring with it terrific clarity about the basics. Good management works to achieve that same level of clarity, even when there is no comparable pressure to do so. Consider Fidelity Investments' retirement business.

Fidelity is the largest mutual fund company in the United States, with over $800 billion in managed assets. Companies like Fidelity make money by charging a management fee tied to the value of the assets they manage. Simply put, the more money that's invested with them, and the more the value of those assets increases, the more money they make. During the 1990s, the retirement business grew from being a small part of Fidelity's business to over 30 percent of it, reflecting steady growth in both the number of account holders and the dollar value of the assets under management.

Sounds like success. However, those measures alone "would only tell us that we've grown, and that we're more important within Fidelity than we used to be," says Ellyn McColgan, who headed one of Fidelity's retirement companies. "They tell us little about how we were doing against our mission." What's the *real* bottom line for Fidelity's retirement business? Answering that question meant going beyond obvious measures, such as assets under management, the number of participants and profitability. "For all of those indicators to stay healthy over the long run," McColgan says, "we *really* have to care about our mission, which is to make sure people who invest with Fidelity will have enough money to retire. If they don't ultimately assets, and participants and profits will all decline. It may take a while, but it will happen."

"Making sure that Americans have enough money to retire" is a very different mission from, say, "Having the biggest market share in the retirement business." Clarity about mission lets McColgan monitor the right measures. "We do know something about what it takes to have enough money for retirement," she explains. "For example, it's not a good thing for a young person to be 100 percent invested in fixed income, or for a participant in his peak earning years to fail to maximize his deferral. But it's a very good thing for a preretiree to calculate his income needs. So, we track these measures and take action to improve them. We proactively seek out participants who appear to be underinvested. We work with plan sponsors to assess asset allocation and portfolio diversification for their participants. We offer planning tools to help people establish financial goals and measure progress against them." Mission, in short, is translated into relevant measures, and those measures are translated into action.

Dell Computer's measures for translating its mission into performance are equally fine grained and altogether different. When Michael Dell founded his company in 1984, his purpose was simple: to give customers a better deal by selling to them directly instead of going through a middleman, as the rest of industry then did. Working as a one-man operation from his college dorm room, Michael Dell had no need to articulate this purpose or to explain how the business worked. To become the industry giant Dell is today, however, he had to make the organization's purpose concrete. This meant defining results and specifying measures of performance that would keep a large organization focused on the right things.

In Dell's case, as you saw earlier, one of the keys to success is speed. More specifically, "speed" refers to the elapsed time between the moment a computer's components are manufactured and the moment a fully assembled computer reaches the customer's desktop. Why does speed matter? In the computer business, new products are introduced so rapidly that if you have old components, even if they are just several months old, chances are those machines will be obsolete before they get to market. When that happens, the computer maker simply has to sell them at a deep discount and swallow the loss. The expense of obsolete inventory is a fact of life in any business where the product life cycle is short—whether the business is computers or fashion.

Very early on, Dell made the connection between its business model and its performance measures. Dell and his managers were able to translate what they were trying to do—give customers the best available technology at the lowest possible cost—into concrete metrics. For example, Dell discovered that the more often a component, a monitor, say, was touched by a Dell worker, the longer the assembly process took and the more likely it was that the final computer would have a quality problem. So, Dell began to measure "touches," and set about systematically to reduce the number. For its monitors, Dell ultimately drove this number to zero. Working with its supplier, Sony, whose quality rates are high, Dell was able to put its name on the monitors without ever taking them out of the box. As Michael Dell explains, "What's the point in having a monitor put on a truck to Austin, Texas and taken off the truck and sent on a little tour around the warehouse, only to be put back on another truck?"

The imperative of speed was translated into Dell's financial strategy as well. One problem that plagues most growing companies, even profitable ones, is that, if they're not careful, they can run out of cash. (This is why start-ups often worry about *burn rates*, which is a measure of how fast a company is using up its seed money.) Thomas J. Meredith, Dell's former CFO, was an architect of the company's effort to solve the problem of financing rapid growth. The question is simple: How do you balance rapid growth with profitability and liquidity? *Gross margin*, which is revenue minus the cost of goods sold, is a traditional measure of profitability. It doesn't include, however, all the funds that have to be invested in growth (advertising to build your market, for example, and money invested in facilities and inventory). Meredith shifted Dell's financial focus from gross margin to *return on invested capital,* a measure that includes those funds, paving the way for Dell's focus on low-inventory manufacturing. In fact, his car's license plate was ROIC, which may seem silly, but is very telling. If you want thousands of people to march in the same direction, some symbolism and theatrics are usually required.

Dell wanted to grow fast, and to do so without taking on a lot of debt to fund its working capital. To this end, one of the things they did was measure *days inventory,* a ratio that tells you how long it would take to draw down the inventory you have. (It's the number of units on hand divided by the number of units sold per day.) Dell focused everyone in the organization on coming up with ideas to get that number lower and lower. Why? The less inventory a company has, the less money it ties up carrying it.

Changing Measures at GE

Under Jack Welch's leadership, GE's performance has been consistently outstanding for twenty years. What measures did Welch use? It all depended on the state of the company and the state of the global economy. During his years as CEO, Welch moved the company through several phases, each marked by a simple theme and a phrase that could be repeated over and over, coupled with related measures. Because GE is a conglomerate, the themes were broad, and the measures were chosen so that they could be applied across many businesses, each with its own business model and strategy. By setting overarching goals for where GE's revenues and profits should come from, Welch shifted GE's emphasis from manufacturing to service, and transformed it from a U.S. company to a global player.

Welch began GE's transformation in the 1980s with clear strategic measures. Convinced that success had left the company's management too internally focused and in need of shaking up, he demanded that every GE business be the number-one or number-two player in its market, a lesson Welch learned from Peter Drucker. Market leaders, by virtue of their greater market power and scale, were more likely to achieve superior performance. If you weren't number one or number two you had to fix the business, or else close it or sell it. "Fix, close, sell" was the simple message that told everybody where GE was headed. Welch began with strategy rather than execution, choosing a measure that forced people to face the reality of their business's competitive position and its prospects for superior performance.

In the 1990s, having restructured (and demoralized) GE, Welch shifted to productivity measures as a way of refocusing on the basics and rebuilding morale and confidence. To win, Welch now said, "we have to find the key to dramatic, sustained productivity growth." His overarching message to the organization was "Speed, Simplicity, Self-Confidence." To make the slogan concrete, Welch focused on a handful of key measures, which included three "to live by: customer satisfaction, employee satisfaction, and cash flow. High customer satisfaction means you're going to get market share. Satisfied employees will be productive employees. And if you've got cash in the till at the end, the rest is all going to work."

Then, in the mid-1990s, Welch replaced the number-one, number-two rule with a new strategic goal. He challenged GE's business leaders to redefine their markets broadly—in such a way that they didn't have more than 10 percent of the market—and to lay out a plan for growth. Why the shift? Welch understood that any "hard and fast rule . . . is too easy to get around." People in organizations are very creative when it comes to gaming performance systems—and so the lines need to be redrawn periodically. Welch realized that, over time, GE's managers had learned how to redefine markets narrowly so that they came out number-one or number-two. Welch's new challenge forced them to focus on growth.

In 1996, Welch began his six sigma crusade. The measure itself, as we've explained, is a quality measure. But as it's practiced at GE, six sigma is a program that captures all the elements of value creation, because it takes a systems approach to the business. The process begins with asking the customer to define the value he wants (in other words, it starts with an outside–in perspective). Then, GE aligns every element of its process, from product design to manufacture to selling and distribution, so that the system is tailored to create the value customers want.

Welch was obsessive about six sigma, characteristically combining numeric measures with broad themes to focus all of GE's three hundred thousand-plus employees on a common goal. For example, he created a new "warrior class" of green belts, black belts, and master black belts, based on increasing levels of training and accomplishment. He also made proficiency in six sigma a requirement for promotion within GE, thereby sending another clear message as well: Get with the program or you don't belong here.

What's the Bottom Line When There Is No Bottom Line?

The belief that mission and the bottom line are hopelessly at odds is widespread, especially in the social sector, where there is no literal bottom line. The basis for this misconception is a logical fallacy that goes something like this:

Mission = People.

Bottom Line = Profits.

People ≠ Profits.

Therefore, Mission ≠ Bottom Line.

This logic is fundamentally flawed and self-defeating. Rather than being antithetical to mission, performance is all about realizing the mission. Performance and mission are never in conflict, *if* performance is properly understood and defined. In fact, whether we're talking about a business or a nonprofit organization, performance is impossible without a mission.

Museums used to see themselves as cultural custodians, repositories for conserving valuable objects. Given that mission, the contents of the institution's collection and the value of its holdings might be appropriate measures of performance. Today, however, most museums have a radically different mission. Now, most see themselves as cultural advocates, expanding the audience for inspiration, beauty, and taste. However, cultural advocacy can take many forms, and how success is defined will affect the behavior of the museum staff. If expanding the audience is the primary objective, the focus will be on increasing the number of visitors, which will encourage curators to create shows that are aimed very broadly. If the goal is building a loyal clientele of genuine patrons, you might track the frequency of visits (the museum's version of repeat sales) or the number of museum memberships sold. Defining performance in this way makes the objective clear to everyone.

As another example, suppose you're running a hospital emergency room. How do you define success? Repeat sales would surely not be the measure. On the contrary, repeat sales in an emergency room usually mean that people with no doctors and no health insurance are using the emergency room for their primary health needs. This is almost always a terrible thing for everyone involved. It's bad health care for the patient, and bad for the hospital's bottom line. So, what is the right measure for an emergency room: how fast people are seen, the number of heart-attack victims who survive the first few hours after arrival, or something else altogether?

Many nonprofit organizations measure their success by their efforts and not their impact. Foundations, for example, report the number of grants they've awarded, but how many of them track the outcomes those grants were designed to produce? Police departments often count the number of officers walking the neighborhoods, or how many emergency calls they answer. Shifting the emphasis from measuring police activity to measuring results was a major element of the reorganization of the New York City

Police Department in the mid-1990s. For Commissioner William Bratton, the bottom line was reducing crime.

The NYPD began an intensive focus on crime statistics, not just, in the words of one senior staff member, "as a way of keeping score at the end of the year, but as a means of managing for results." Consistent with the NYPD's new broken-windows theory of change, the precinct commanders were held accountable for new metrics: for example, the proportion of people arrested and searched in connection with misdemeanors. Bratton and his team used these metrics to track the department's progress toward the ultimate goal—reducing crime. The measures served to align everyone's behavior with that mission.

Translating purpose into performance measures is a very subtle, very complex task. It is anything but a sterile, uncreative, numerical exercise, as the experience of The Nature Conservancy illustrates. Year by year, the number of acres under its protection had increased, membership had risen, and donations had grown. By their traditional measures of "bucks" and "acres," TNC was achieving superior performance. But the organization's purpose, its mission, is to save plant and animal species. While they were raising more money and buying more land, they were losing the bigger war for biodiversity. Led by John Sawhill, the organization stopped in 1990 to rethink both its strategy and the measures they were using to define success.

Having acquired a property called Schenob Brook in Massachusetts, TNC was alarmed to find that the bog turtle population was declining. "Activities outside our preserve were affecting the water that the turtles ultimately depended on. Here was the problem: We thought we could buy a piece of land, fence it off, and thereby protect whatever was in that preserve. But that thinking proved mistaken, which meant that our old performance measures—such as how much land we had acquired for conservation—weren't valid indicators of institutional progress. We simply couldn't go on with business-as-usual. For-profit companies can look at their financial statements every day to see how they're doing: They're either making money or they're not. Without the discipline of the bottom line, it's easier for nonprofit organizations to get off track. For the Conservancy, science is really our bottom line."

And science pointed the way to new measures of performance. Now, every project the Conservancy undertakes defines and/or tracks five key elements of success: the ecological system it's trying to protect, the stresses to that system, the source of the stresses, the strategy for dealing with them, and how to measure success. The Conservancy's Fish Creek Project in northeastern Indiana, which is working to protect a system of freshwater mussels, is a good example. The stress comes from excessive silt in the water, which comes from two agricultural practices: tillage up to the water's edge and fall plowing. TNC has been helping farmers practice no-till agriculture by subsidizing their equipment costs. For this project, TNC is using three measures of success: the number of acres under the no-till method, the silt levels in the water, and the size of the mussel population in Fish Creek. "Ultimately," says Sawhill, "we have to measure success by the species we save. But in the short term, to find out if we're on the right track, we have to learn what we should be monitoring."

Organizations like TNC that are grounded in science may have a leg up in the difficult task of finding performance measures that capture their mission. For the most part, organizations in the social sector have a better handle on inputs than they do on outcomes. In education, for example, it's a whole lot easier to measure what you put into schooling—the number of classrooms and libraries, the hours of teaching, which courses should be required—than it is to define what kind of person you want the educational system to produce. If the real result of education is a productive citizen, how do you measure success?

It's very easy to call for accountability and results when you're a politician running for office. It is a lot harder if you're a high school principal trying to please a community that doesn't agree about the underlying purpose of public education, much less the measures used to define performance. The current debate over the state of public education in the United States attests to the difficulty. The lesson of management is clear. Improving the quality of education means first agreeing on what you're trying to accomplish, then translating that purpose into concrete measures of performance.

The right measures and goals can help organizations of all sorts achieve their purposes. Broadly speaking, the challenge facing the social sector is increasingly the challenge of advanced economies. The more that knowledge work replaces physical labor, the output of which can be easily weighed and measured, and the more our economy tilts toward services and intangibles, the more thoughtful organizations must be about how they define their aspirations and measure their performance.

Chapter 7

Betting on the Future: Innovation and Uncertainty

Behold the turtle, He only makes progress when he sticks his neck out.

—James Bryant Conant (1893–1978)
President, Harvard University

Like the navigators of the age of exploration, good managers always have one eye fixed on the horizon and the other on their current position. They are accountable for results now—this quarter—and at the same time they are responsible for the long term. How do managers live simultaneously in two time zones? In most instances, very uncomfortably.

Managers either innovate today or fall behind tomorrow. But every dollar they spend for the future is charged against today's performance. So, they are constantly robbing Peter to pay Paul, knowing all the while that they need to stay on friendly terms with both of them.

Moreover, there is no guarantee that their investments will ever pay off. By definition, the future is uncertain. That is why investments in innovation are often likened to bets at the racetrack. It's a helpful metaphor, as long as you keep the differences in mind. To begin with, management has to create its own bets. That's the work of *innovation*, a very special kind of problem solving. It's the search for new ways to create value, and new value to create. Organizations with better information and better insights about value get to make bets that aren't available to their rivals. Second, management actively works its bets to change the odds in its favor. At the track, you don't get to do that. If you want to play, you have to accept the house odds and, once the race begins, all you can do is wait passively for the outcome.

This chapter explains how the discipline of management tackles the risky business of innovation. It is about how management gathers and uses information to create better bets, to make smarter choices among competing bets, and to manage bets once they've been placed.

Juggling the Present and the Future

In May 1927, Henry Ford did a most extraordinary thing. He shut down his assembly line and sent the workers home while he went back to the drawing board. It remains one of the colossal ironies of history: the man who as much as any single individual invented the future got stuck in the past. He failed to grasp that the very success of the Model T would make it obsolete. Had Ford been less wedded to his own creation, he would have seen the wave of change coming. Instead, he was forced to close the world's most famous industrial facility.

What Ford didn't count on was that once he had introduced people to automobile ownership, he would change their lives forever. Ford, remember, made cars affordable for the mass market. This meant that someone buying a car was almost surely buying his *first* car. Ford never imagined that when it came time for a *second* car, or a *third*, people would develop a taste for better cars, for more comfort and power and style—which is precisely what happened. The growing prosperity of the nation, coupled with the rise of installment buying, meant more people could afford those better cars.

It also meant that their first cars were now available for resale as used cars. So, the Model T, which once owned the basic transportation end of the market, was undercut by a flood of even lower-priced used cars. Ford's rival Alfred Sloan describes the shift: "When first-car buyers returned to the market for the second round, with the old car as a first payment on a new car, they were selling basic transportation and demanding something more than that in the new car."

Ford should have seen the end coming in 1925. That year, his volume held steady at two million cars and trucks. But since the market was growing fast, Ford's share plummeted from 54 to 45 percent. The next year, Chevrolet took even more ground from Ford. By May 1927, Ford had to admit that the game was up. He sent his workers home while he developed the successor to the Model T.

Ford's myopia wasn't fatal. His company survived. Others have paid more dearly. Consider the recent demise of the Digital Equipment Corporation (DEC), whose founder was so wedded to minicomputers that, as late as 1977, he couldn't envision individuals wanting to have computers in their homes. A decade later, what was left of DEC was acquired by Compaq.

Major discontinuities, like the shift to PCs, are always treacherous. It's no secret that biotechnology will cast a very long shadow in the twenty-first century, just as chemistry did in the twentieth century. But that sweeping generalization won't help companies know exactly when to reallocate their resources. Monsanto, once a major chemicals company, bet its future on biotechnology. It appeared that Monsanto got the technology right, developing a range of products that promised to raise the productivity of agriculture with less environmental damage than a chemicals-based approach. Develop plants with a genetic resistance to pests, for example, and farmers won't have to spray their fields with tons of chemical pesticides. But Monsanto's CEO, Robert Shapiro, who may one day be hailed as a visionary, lost his company and his job because he underestimated the political reaction to genetically modified crops. The technology was ready, but the market wasn't. The end came when Monsanto was acquired by Pharmacia. In another five to ten years we'll know whether Shapiro was a man ahead of his time, or a deluded dreamer.

Juggling the present and the future is the dilemma 120-year-old Kodak faces as it prepares to enter a new era of digital photography. The question isn't whether Kodak will make the transition, but how and when. In 1999, over 80 percent of Kodak's revenue and just about all of its earnings came from traditional imaging. As digital cameras begin to sell in large numbers, and as growth accelerates, Kodak is spending $500 million a year on digital research and development (R&D), bringing in new executives with relevant expertise, and redrawing its organizational lines. Its real challenge is getting positioned for the digital era without writing off its profitable traditional businesses too soon.

Radical shifts in markets and technologies—like Monsanto's and Kodak's—represent an extreme. But the underlying dilemma, the precarious balancing act between the present and the future, is the universal condition of management. And that's true for non-profit organizations as well, odd as that might appear at first blush. Nonprofit organizations face such overwhelming pressure to devote every penny they have to direct service, to *today's* programs, that investment in the capability to achieve greater social impact tomorrow is crowded out. The service ethic is so powerful that we tend to think of nonprofits simply as conduits that transfer resources from funders to beneficiaries. Few funders, or even managers in the sector, for that matter, appreciate that without investments today in organization-building and innovation, there won't be improved capacity to do better tomorrow.

Organizations of all sorts, then, need disciplines to propel them into the future, to push back against the pressures of today. Otherwise, says Andy Grove, we are likely "to do too little too late." He notes, "With all the rhetoric about how management is about change, the fact is that we managers loathe change, especially when it involves us." 3M, a company much admired for its track record of innovation, has long required that each division generate at least 25 percent of its sales from products or services introduced in the past five years. In 1993, as the pace of competition quickened, 3M upped the requirement to 30 percent and four years. The specific numbers 3M has chosen may be somewhat arbitrary, but the need for mechanisms and incentives to force us into the future is not.

Good Management Is Entrepreneurial

Managing for the long term, then, takes discipline, as well as a certain amount of courage. Perhaps more than anything else, though, it takes a radical belief in the promise of tomorrow. At the end of World War II, Hewlett-Packard's defense contracts suddenly dried up, cutting HP's revenues in half. To save their fledgling company, Bill Hewlett and David Packard had to let people go. At the same time, however, they saw an opportunity. Other companies were laying off some of the industry's most talented engineers. Hewlett and Packard scooped them up, believing in a brighter future at a time when things looked pretty bleak.

The investments that managers make to project their organizations into the future, whether it's hiring people they're not sure they can afford or developing new products, reflect the fundamental optimism of management. In the nineteenth century, economics picked up a nickname it has been unable to shake. It was dubbed "the dismal science," because Thomas Malthus predicted that population growth would outstrip society's ability to produce life's essentials. At its core, management's disposition is not just anti-Malthusian, it is relentlessly upbeat and self-confident. There's no problem that can't be solved, no status quo that can't be bettered.

We tend to associate this forward-looking, change-seeking attitude with entrepreneurs, not managers. Increasingly, however, we have come to understand that good management must be entrepreneurial. In the boom years following World War II, growth was like riding a wave: If the market was growing (in size and affluence) and you had a place in it, you would grow as well. Today's economy is different, and so is our understanding of where growth comes from. Economists like Paul Romer have demonstrated that innovation and new ideas are the more powerful drivers of growth.

Led by managers who pursue innovation in a disciplined, organized, and purposeful way, the United States has become an entrepreneurial society where change is accepted as the norm. Unlike other social institutions—family and community, for example—which are conservative in nature, the modern organization is a destabilizer, designed to produce change. Truly disruptive ideas may be more likely to come from upstart organizations with no stake in the status quo. It took a Starbucks, for example, to teach the entrenched coffee giants like Nestlé that there was a premium taste market waiting to be served. But incumbents have substantial advantages on their side and, today, most embrace innovation—creating the future—as a top priority.

Contrary to the popular stereotype, then, management and entrepreneurship are not antithetical roles. As Peter Drucker has argued for decades, they "are only two different dimensions of the same task." An entrepreneur who doesn't learn how to manage won't last long. Nor will a manager last long if he doesn't learn to innovate. Lone inventors, the creative geniuses working in their garages, will always have a special place in the American imagination. But the innovation that fuels the growth of most organizations is the product of joint effort, and of a far more disciplined approach. Although no one can be taught to be a creative genius, we can all learn to practice innovation.

Thinking *Inside* the Box

Much of that discipline is captured by a phrase that today makes many people cringe. Sometime around 1990, give or take a few years, we were all admonished to *think outside the box*. Since then, the phrase has entered the lexicon of buzzwords. Usually there is an inverse correlation between the frequency of its use and the amount of truly original thinking underway.

Whenever a phrase like this makes the rounds in organizations, there's usually a genuine itch that needs to be scratched—at least at first. A decade or so ago, overcoming resistance to change was *the* challenge facing organizations of all sorts. The competitive environment had intensified rapidly, and people in large organizations were slow to embrace new ways of thinking.

The problem with phrases like *thinking outside the box* is that they quickly become slogans, applied universally and somewhat mindlessly. That's a shame because, properly understood, *thinking outside the box* can be a very useful metaphor for communicating how ordinary people actually create extraordinary value when they put their heads together in organizations.

The phrase comes from a famous puzzle in mathematics known as the *nine-dot problem*. Visualize a page with nine dots arrayed in three rows of three dots each. Now here's the problem: without lifting your pencil from the page, connect all of the dots by drawing four straight lines. (See the drawing.)

The puzzle stumps us because, when we look at the dots, we immediately see a square. The familiar pattern is inescapable. Most people then unconsciously assume, as they try to solve the puzzle, that they have to stay within the confines of that imaginary square box. Not so. The solution requires that three of the four lines extend *outside* the space defined by the outermost dots. (See the solution.) Hence, *thinking outside the box* as a metaphor for thinking beyond the common mental models that shape the way we see the world.

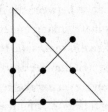

Most people who talk about thinking outside the box are unaware of the phrase's origin. It has come to mean *think creatively!* Or, worse, *dammit, why can't you be more creative?*, an exhortation that leaves most people feeling inadequate and at sea. The phrase alone, divorced from its origins, places a misleading premium on originality for its own sake. In fact, a lot of valuable innovation is sparked precisely because there is a box and there are constraints that limit and define good solutions—not lifting your pencil, for example. Although we don't usually think of creative artists as problem solvers, much great art finds new solutions within a set of specific and often fairly narrow constraints. Shakespeare's sonnets, for example, are marvelous in part because he was working within and against the constraints of the sonnet form. Toyota's development of just-in-time inventory management was sparked by the company's cramped physical space.

Anyone who has seen the film version of the *Apollo 13* space mission will remember a scene set in a conference room at Mission Control in Houston. An explosion caused by a faulty coil in an oxygen tank has damaged the spacecraft. Landing on the moon— *Apollo 13*'s mission—is out of the question. Gene Kranz, director of flight operations, decisively redirects his organization to a new mission: bringing the crew home alive. The spacecraft is dangerously low on power, and may not have enough to return safely to earth. Mission Control is working against the clock to design an energy-saving reentry plan when another emergency light starts flashing. Carbon-dioxide levels are rising rapidly. If Mission Control can't design a makeshift air filter that the astronauts can cobble together with objects at hand in the space capsule, the astronauts will die. A project leader dumps three boxes full of assorted objects on the table, then says to his team: "We've got to find a way to make *this* (holding up a square object) fit into the hole for *this* (picking up a round object) using nothing but *that* (pointing to the mound of stuff on the table)." The resulting filter—patched together with some plastic hose, duct tape, the cover of the crew's flight plan, and one sock—does the job.

How does Mission Control save the *Apollo 13* astronauts? Passion, dedication, the refusal to accept failure—all of these play their part. But they would not have prevailed without the organization's disciplined clarity about goals and constraints. Everyone is focused on the problem they have to solve. Do they find creative solutions rapidly to seemingly impossible problems? Yes. Are they thinking outside the box? You could say *yes*, but only if you understand that doing so depends on absolute clarity about the box—the problem to be solved and the constraints that must be respected. Gene Kranz defines the box for Mission Control by restating their overriding purpose, incorporating real-time data about the harsh realities of the astronauts' situation, the power shortage, the rising CO_2 levels. These are the critical and often underappreciated disciplines of problem solving.

The essence of innovating, of creating new value, is solving problems within constraints—Eastman's $25 Kodak camera versus the one-dollar Brownie. Good managers know how to use the constraints of strategy, constraints of a business model, constraints of a budget, to set them as challenges that spark creativity and ingenuity. This is a key discipline of effective innovation.

David Pottruck, co-CEO of Charles Schwab, tells a story that illustrates this discipline in action. A team was asked to find a better way to research and resolve customer complaints—a less heroic mission than Houston's, but more like the work of incremental innovation that most of us engage in. First, the team mapped out Schwab's process and found ways to shave a couple of days off the two-week total. Next, adopting a more aggressive goal—reduce the time to one week—prompted better analysis of the process. Everyone took for granted, for example, that contacting customers in writing was a legal requirement. It turned out that letters, which added days to the process, were a matter of custom, not law. By phoning, Schwab saved another big chunk of time.

Soon, the team had the time down to a week but, instead of declaring victory and stopping, it posed a bolder question: Can we get the response time down to forty-eight hours? This wasn't incremental problem solving anymore, it was redefining the problem altogether. It was starting all over again with fresh thinking about the value the process created. In other words, it was redefining the box. At this point, all of the givens were up for grabs. What did customers want? That had seemed clear. They wanted quick response time. But wait a minute. Didn't they *really* want their complaints resolved in their favor? What would Schwab do differently if the problem were redefined as customer retention instead of complaint response? That question—and the insight about value that provoked it—led the Schwab team to ask what it would cost to give customers what they truly wanted. Answering that question meant analyzing how much Schwab was spending to resolve each dispute.

The team discovered that 80 percent of the complaints involved dollar amounts that were less than what Schwab was spending to research them. So, if the goal is to retain customers, why not simply concede any dispute in which the dollar amount in question is less than that cost? Reframing the question turned incremental improvement into a breakthrough, allowing Schwab to settle 80 percent of the disputes in forty-eight hours. To complete the story, Schwab changed the department's performance measures—from complaint response to customer retention—so that everyone would understand the *real* bottom line.

Was this thinking outside the box? Again, yes and no. Reframing the question was essentially a process of describing a new box with a new set of carefully defined constraints. Although successful managers may use different metaphors to talk about what they do, at its core, the innovative work of organizations is the orchestrated search for new value. This is management in its entrepreneurial mode, creating a more productive future. Thinking inside the box of value helps you step outside the box of your past mindset.

The Information You Need

Where, then, do new insights about value come from? How do you get the information you need to draw the box? The answer—begun in our chapter on value creation—is that you get it by looking through the customer's eyes, from the outside in. That's the concept. Now, here's the execution.

The familiar phrase *listening to customers*, doesn't fully capture what's going on. Gathering the information you need to create better bets requires active engagement, not just passive listening. It requires you to actively suspend your own intuition, to observe how other people behave, and without imposing your own logic, to ask why.

This takes discipline because it goes against the grain in a number of ways. Most people prefer talking to listening. The more successful they've been, the more in danger they are of believing that when it comes to their business, they know best. True curiosity about other people—a passionate interest in understanding *why* people do what they do—is rare. Suspending judgment, observation, and curiosity—these are the necessary complements (and sometimes antidotes) to the prompting of instinct, intuition, and industry lore.

The popular image of market research as a statistical black box that magically answers all questions doesn't do justice to the art of discovering needs that customers themselves often don't know that they have. The process of gathering information and developing new insights owes a good deal to the methods of cultural anthropology. In the "Strategy" chapter, we described Pepsi's clever gamesmanship in introducing plastic bottles, an innovation that put Coke between a rock and a hard place. Now, let's look at how Pepsi arrived at that new insight about value.

In the 1970s, Pepsi had fallen well behind Coke in the U.S. cola market. Determined to find a way to gain the lead, the Pepsi marketers began to study how people behaved when they bought and consumed soft drinks. In one study, 350 families were able to purchase as much soda as they wanted each week, at discounted prices. When the researchers followed their subjects' behavior at home, they discovered something no one had anticipated: The only limit to the amount of soda people would drink was the amount they could carry home.

On the basis of this insight, Pepsi began to focus on packaging and, more specifically, on making its bottles as light and portable as possible. They introduced plastic in place of glass and multi-packs instead of six-packs. The result is visible on every supermarket shelf in the world. Such an innovation never would have come from the intuition of marketers at Coke or Pepsi. (It would have been particularly unthinkable for Coke, because its distinctive hour-glass-shaped green bottle was so strongly identified with the brand.) Nor would the innovation have come by asking customers what they wanted. It resulted, instead, from an insight into another person's experience, from watching with an open mind and having the curiosity to ask why.

There's so much focus on the role of creativity in innovation that it overshadows our appreciation of the power of curiosity. When Jack Welch anointed Jeff Immelt to succeed him as GE's CEO, it was probably no accident that Welch cited his successor's love of change and his curiosity in the same breath. Ray Kroc, the founder of McDonald's, was a veteran milk-shake salesman, and he knew that most restaurants needed only one or two machines, because each could make five shakes at a time. Why, then, he wondered, was a restaurant in San Bernardino, California, owned by a couple of brothers named McDonald buying eight of these machines? What kind of operation could possibly churn out forty milk shakes at a time? Kroc just had to see for himself what was going on. His visit to the McDonald brothers in 1954 resulted in a new industry.

The same spirit of curiosity underlies the history of innovation at 3M. In 1920, Francis Okie, a manufacturer of printers' inks in Philadelphia, sent a letter out to a number of mineral and sandpaper companies requesting "samples of every mineral grit size you use in manufacturing sandpaper." Since 3M didn't sell raw materials, it didn't imagine Okie would become a customer. But 3M's CEO, William McKnight, "curiosity piqued and on the prowl for interesting new ideas that might move the company forward—asked a simple question: '*Why* does Mr. Okie want these samples?'" None of the other companies Okie contacted bothered to ask that question. Okie's answer led McKnight to acquire the rights to one of 3M's most important products of all time, Wetordry, a waterproof sandpaper, and to hire Okie himself.

Similarly, a number of innovations at Schwab have come from watching how people behave, and asking why. Why, for example, was its TeleBroker so popular with customers whose native language wasn't English? TeleBroker is a touch-tone, fully automated brokerage system that provides quotes and executes trades. Watching who used Telebroker and how, Schwab discovered an unmet need. For someone whose English wasn't strong, using the system was easier than speaking to a live associate. The real need, then, was for segmented language-specific services for Chinese- and Spanish-speaking customers, which Schwab subsequently introduced.

Sometimes, you have to take what people say with a grain of salt, especially when they say one thing and do another. When asked about the importance of local branches, Schwab's customers typically reply that they're not very important. Yet, says Pottruck, every time the company opens a new branch, new business in that community doubles. This is especially vexing because it flies in the face of Internet wisdom, which would direct Schwab to avoid the fixed costs associated with physical branches. Yet, the data says that even as Schwab does 80 percent of its transactions electronically, 70 percent of its new accounts are opened in branch offices, through face-to-face contact. Clearly, Pottruck says, local human presence is important, but somehow the phrase *branch office* on a survey doesn't trigger the response. "The science of market research," he concludes, "has to be interpreted by a human being in the real world."

Making Decisions About an Uncertain Future

What we've been discussing so far are ways of collecting, sorting, and sifting through information that will help you to create better bets about the future. With the right information, you will be able to stack the odds in your favor. However, even with the best information in the world, you can't know the future.

Business success stories, when looked at in hindsight, always have a sense of inevitability about them. When you hear about Hewlett and Packard scooping up talented engineers after World War II, at a time they could scarcely afford to pay their rent, you can almost anticipate the next sentence: " . . . and the rest is history. Those hires fueled HP's extraordinary growth for decades to come." But as the historian David McCullough likes to remind us, there is nothing fixed and inevitable about history. Although history is "the past," the people who made that history were living in their own lively and confusing present. Their ventures, far from being inevitable, could have turned out differently.

The fact that things can turn out in more ways than one is perhaps the defining characteristic of managerial decision making. You are forced to commit resources today toward performance in an uncertain future. And, although the money you plunk down today is hard cash, the future stream is both a hope and a guess. There is no guarantee it will ever materialize.

What that stream of payments actually turns out to be will depend on many things. With a well-established business, or an investment that resembles many others you've made in the past, the near term may seem like familiar and predictable territory. With a new venture, even next quarter can be highly uncertain. For both new and old, the further out in time you try to project that earnings stream, the greater the chance that the unexpected will happen: technology or customer tastes will change, new competitors will emerge, a recession will set in, and so on. The only thing you can count on is that you won't have all the information you need to make a decision and, yet, you will have to decide. At some point, you will have to take a leap of faith, as Bill Hewlett and David Packard did.

A lot of life's important decisions require you to act on the basis of incomplete information and make bets that can't be recalled once they are placed. This is almost universally true about the decisions managers are forced to make every day. Author and longtime investment advisor Peter Bernstein offers up a witty summary of the problem, which could be titled "The Innovator's Lament":
the information you have isn't what you want;
the information you want isn't the information you need;
the information you need isn't the information you can obtain;
the information you can obtain costs more than you're willing to pay

Part of the discipline of innovation, then, involves parsing the information you have. What are facts, as opposed to assumptions, as opposed to assertions? What is knowable and what isn't? Is the outcome very sensitive to information you don't have? If the answer to that last question is *yes*, can you get that information from pilot projects and experiments before you have to make big commitments? How representative or relevant is the information you have? Sampling isn't just for statisticians. We all make decisions about the future based on some partial information from the past. If you liked one book by John Grisham, you assume you'll like the next one, for example. These questions about the future don't require a crystal ball. They require skills of logic.

When Schwab opens a new branch or Starbucks enters a new market, neither can know in advance how many new customers will show up, but they can know plenty of other relevant facts. They can know, for example, what kind of people use their services, and choose locations that will increase the odds of attracting them. They can know what a new outlet will cost and, therefore, how many new customers they will need to cover those costs. (This technique is called *break-even analysis*.) Using their experience and their best judgment, they can then ask themselves whether that seems like a reasonable number to expect.

If there were no uncertainty, there would be no need to make decisions—you would just do it. Faced with an uncertainty they can't resolve, good managers ask themselves simple questions: What do we have to believe about x to push forward with this initiative? And then: Are those reasonable things to believe?

Which Bets to Place

Nothing ventured, nothing gained. The phrase dates back to the sixteenth century, to an age when a new commercial class was risking its fortunes at sea. Recall Shakespeare's *Merchant of Venice*. Almost four hundred years before the Nobel Prize was awarded to Harry Markowitz for working out the intricacies of portfolio theory, Shakespeare's merchant grasped the importance of diversifying his risk. His valuable cargo was carried on a half-dozen ships, each bound for a different port. He knew better than to put all his eggs in one basket.

Merchants like Antonio had an intuitive grasp of value, probability, and risk, even if the capital market on the Venetian Rialto left something to be desired. (In lieu of interest, Antonio pledges a pound of his flesh to Shylock if he is unable to repay the loan.) All decision making under uncertainty—even this bizarre deal—involves some calculation of consequences and probabilities. People know when they buy their lottery tickets that the odds are terrible. But, oh, those consequences! It's a sucker's bet, of course, but most lottery players feel they pay a small price for a big dream.

Greed and fear are the twin demons that cloud our judgments about risk and return. *Risk aversion* is the more common problem: Paralyzed by the fear of loss, we avoid taking even the most reasonable of chances. Lotteries depend on a different psychology: Blinded by the disproportionate size of the reward, we underestimate the risk.

Managers can't afford to sit on the sidelines, so they have to be more clearheaded and disciplined about the bets they place. The entrepreneurial work of management is not just a crapshoot, even though a casino mentality periodically takes hold on Wall Street. Today's managers have at their disposal a set of simple but powerful tools for structuring decisions involving uncertainty. Taught under a variety of headings—quantitative methods, finance, decision science, and negotiation—they provide a systematic way to deal with the unknown. They make it possible for the average merchant or entrepreneur to make smarter choices about the future, choices about which bets to place and how to place them.

What's It Worth?

New opportunities to create value always come with a price tag. William Clay Ford, Henry's great grandson and the company's current chairman, is investing $2 billion to turn Ford's River Rouge facility into an environmental showcase, and he's betting hundreds of millions of dollars on more fuel-efficient cars and trucks. Those investments will create value only if they are worth more than they cost. That much is obvious. Putting a value on an outcome you hope to achieve and figuring in the cost of the risk you're taking is not at all obvious, however. Those questions have occupied some of the best minds in finance for the past half century.

The cost of capital, which can sound very abstract, is as real and concrete as the cost of labor and steel. It is basically the cost of using other people's money in a risky enterprise. The riskier the undertaking, the more compensation investors and lenders will require. The cost of capital, then, is part of the price you pay to create the future.

Before we had personal computers and handheld calculators, managers relied on a seat-of-the-pants approach to investment decisions. As a simple proxy for risk and return, they adopted a measure called *payback*. If you put $10 million into a plant that would generate $2 million a year in new profits, it would take you five years to recover your initial investment. Payback analysis has the virtue of simplicity, but it ignores risk, and it ignores the fact that alternative investments have different time horizons and face different sorts of uncertainties. Like all performance measures, payback has its own built-in biases. If it's the only yardstick you use, you will systematically (and inadvertently) favor shorter-term initiatives.

One of the most important ideas in finance—and the one that more than any other shapes the way organizations make judgments about consequences—is a measure called *net present value* (NPV). NPV is the price you'd be willing to pay today to buy all the net cash flows associated with an investment. It is the answer to the fundamental question: *What's it worth?*

To calculate the net present value of an investment, we first have to *discount* all of the future cash flows to reflect the simple fact that tomorrow's dollar is worth less than today's, and the added fact that there may be some risk to the payments. (This is called *discounted cash flow* analysis, or DCF.) Then we *net out*, or subtract, the present value of the dollars invested from the present value of the dollars returned. A positive NPV gives you a green light. It tells you that, after adjusting for the riskiness of the undertaking, you'll get back more than you invest.

Net present value has been *the* signature tool of professional managers for the past three decades. It has become the global standard. The calculation is too cumbersome to do by hand, but became feasible with the advent of handheld calculators. More than just a tool, however, NPV has become a mindset, a way of seeing the world, and a universal language for talking about valuation.

Answering the question, "what's it worth?" is not simply about plugging numbers into a spreadsheet. As you reason backward from the future you're trying to create, you have to ask yourself what success will look like and what resources it will take, over what time frame, to achieve your ambitions. Too often, the tougher questions go unasked—or worse, they are asked perfunctorily, then dismissed. People confuse the *best case* (what they hope will happen) with the *base case* (what's most likely to happen). The cash flows you lay out are only as good as your answers to these questions: What could go wrong? What could go right? How likely is it that those things might happen?

NPV allows managers to project forward with a sense of control. This is its strength, but also its weakness, because sometimes the sense of control is based on the illusion of precision. We think that because the numbers on the page are so specific they must be real. We forget that, like all models, NPV rests on a number of assumptions. First, that you can translate your expectations about future events into a specific forecast of revenues and costs. Second, that you can capture the impact of both time and risk in the discount rate you use to adjust those cash flows. And third, that once you set out on the path those cash flows represent, you won't change your mind along the way.

Recognize these assumptions, and you've got a useful way to structure and quantify many of the investment decisions critical to creating the future. Ignore them, and follow the numbers mindlessly, and you will be emboldened by a false sense of certainty.

NPV has an important limitation as a model of reality. It does not capture the dynamic sequence of learning and acting that characterizes so many strategic investments. A drug company, for example, might invest first in developing a new medicine. But only if the drug works will the company go on to subsequent investments: in facilities to make the drug, in a sales force to sell it, in R&D for the next generation of that drug. DCF doesn't capture the active and flexible way we respond to events in the real world, the way we scale up or back, or shift course entirely, depending on what we learn.

The combination of greater computing power and advances in financial theory have led to the development of an alternative way of valuing investments of this sort. It is based on the method used to establish the price of options. If you think a stock is a good buy, but you're not sure, you can buy a call option that will give you the right to buy that stock in the future at a price you lock in today. Then, you wait for events to unfold, and for more information, before you have to make the more significant commitment of buying the stock itself. Options are a form of insurance. If the stock dips, you've lost only the cost of the option. (Similarly, if your house doesn't burn down, you're out only the cost of your insurance premium.) If the stock rises, you get the upside by exercising your option to buy the stock at the old price.

The concept underlying an option is that there is value in preserving the right to act, value in taking initial steps that might lead to bigger things down the road. There is value in learning, then acting. Option pricing quantifies that value. Increasingly, the thinking that goes into pricing *financial* options like calls or puts is being applied to *real* investments like new plants or drug trials that organizations make for the future.

Xerox, once an icon of corporate America, badly fumbled the future, not because it couldn't innovate, but because it failed to commercialize its innovations. That happened, in part, because it relied on the wrong tools for valuing innovation. In the 1970s, Xerox developed the first personal computer, years before the Apple or the IBM PC. But the Alto, as it was called, was never launched. Xerox's CEO, Archie McCardell, and its head of engineering and manufacturing, Jim O'Neill, were alumni of Ford's finance department—the numbers men assembled by Robert McNamara in the years following World War II.

At Xerox, McCardell and O'Neill created a numbers culture where decisions were put through the NPV test. Not surprisingly, the Alto failed. Like most forays into new technologies or new markets, the Alto couldn't be justified as a standalone investment. Had Xerox seen the Alto as a real option that would allow Xerox to continue to play in the computer business, history might have turned out very differently. Real options remind us that there's value in trying new things and learning, even if your experiments fail. They provide a disciplined but more flexible approach to valuing consequences in the face of uncertainty.

Mapping the Future, Working the Odds

Suppose you were given the choice of two bets. Which one would you choose? (A) A $1 bet with a $25 payoff, or (B) A $1 bet with a $100 payoff. The odds of winning are 1 in 2 for A, 1 in 10 for B.

This is a simple problem. B has the higher payoff but, taking account of the odds, A's the smarter bet. Five times out of ten you'd end up with $25, the other five times you'd be out one dollar. The *expected value* of this bet, the average of the outcomes weighted by their probabilities, is $12. With B, you'd lose your dollar nine times out of ten. The expected value of B is just $9.10. (The weighted average calculation is [.1 x $100] + [.9 x -$1] = $10 - .90 = $9.10.) Creating the future is rarely as simple as placing a bet and waiting passively for the outcome, however. More typically, a number of uncertainties and future choices stand between your initial decision and the outcome you desire. In real life, as opposed to the gaming table, uncertainties are often nested, one within another, and smart decisions take that into account. Moreover, management is active, not passive. You make hundreds of decisions over the course of time as events unfold, as new information emerges, as you learn and respond. At every new decision point, you need to reassess the expected value from that moment forward.

When decisions are sequential, it helps to map them out graphically in the form of a *decision tree*, a versatile tool for thinking systematically about all kinds of decisions—personal as well as business—that involve uncertainty. Constructing a decision tree requires that you think forward from today's decision to the uncertainties that will be resolved over time, and the future decisions you will have to make. A decision tree forces you to think systematically about the order in which spending and learning will occur, and that is enormously useful. Developing new medicines, for example, is risky business. Before a drug can be marketed, it faces a slew of scientific and regulatory risks. A compound that looks promising in the lab may fail in animal trials. (That's one uncertainty resolved.) One that is safe and efficacious in animals may fail in human trials. (That's another.) Or it can get through human trials but fail to win regulatory approval. (That's a third uncertainty.) Drugs that pass all these hurdles then face all the normal risks of competition in the market: that someone else will have a better product, a better sales force, a head start.

Decision trees force you to assign probabilities to every major uncertainty, and to follow the value consequences out to the end of that branch. The exercise is almost always revealing. All of a sudden, out of the fog of events and decisions, you see the iceberg in your path—the one or two key uncertainties with the potential to change the final outcome. For pharmaceuticals, *time to market*—whether you are the first or the second or the third entrant into a new drug category—is always an iceberg. Several companies pursue the same approach to a given problem, whether it's lowering cholesterol, or osteoporosis, or arthritis pain. Whoever gets there first is likely to capture and keep the lion's share of the rewards. Decision analysis helps to quantify just how much it's worth to get to market one month or one year faster.

Put yourself, then, in the shoes of Dr. Edward Scolnick, head of drug research at Merck. In 1994, his company was trailing Monsanto in a high-stakes race to develop and bring to market a new type of painkiller known as COX-2 inhibitors. Monsanto's Celebrex had a significant head start over Merck's Vioxx.

Two promising COX-2 inhibitors survived Merck's initial animal tests for efficacy and safety. The next stage—human trials—is where the drug companies start writing enormous checks. This is where the big bets are placed. What should Dr. Scolnick do? He could test one of the compounds first; if that one failed, he could cycle back and try the second. That would be the cheaper way to go. Alternatively, Scolnick could test both compounds simultaneously. That would be the faster path.

Which path did Scolnick choose? The fast track. It didn't allow Merck to beat Monsanto, but it closed the gap enough to make Vioxx a big success when it did hit the market in 1999. As it turned out, only one of Merck's two compounds worked. "'One failed and the other didn't, and there was no way you could have looked at the pre-clinical data and predicted which one would succeed,' Dr. Scolnick says. 'That's just dumb luck.'"

Dumb luck, yes. Smart decision making, yes. In this case, the bigger bet was the better gamble. So, the decision would have been correct even if Merck had been unlucky and both of its compounds had failed. What this story also shows is that good managers don't just place bets and then wait around to see how things will turn out. Through innovation, they create new opportunities to bet; then they actively work those bets, focusing on the uncertainties that matter most in order to tilt the odds in their favor.

When they can't influence the outcome, as Scolnick was able to do, they might find ways to shed risks that would threaten their success. For example, one of the key determinants of airline profitability is the price of jet fuel. But if you run an airline, there's not a thing you can do to control that price. Instead, a lot of airlines now do what most people do routinely to protect themselves against losses they can't afford—they buy insurance. An airline can buy futures or forward contracts on jet fuel, locking in a future price now, and reducing its exposure to volatile prices that could cripple its performance. As exotic as some of Wall Street's complex contracts for hedging risk have become, they're all basically forms of insurance, allowing companies to manage risk by shedding those they can't afford to carry.

Creating the future is risky business. For managers, that's good news. If there were no uncertainty, there would be few opportunities to create value. With better understanding of value, time, and risk, managers and private individuals can make smarter investment decisions and capital markets can more efficiently fund innovation and growth. We have better tools today for understanding and managing risk, and for decision making in the face of uncertainty, than we have ever had before. These tools help us to see more clearly the tradeoffs between today and tomorrow, and they have contributed to the greater availability of capital that makes tomorrow possible.

Remember, the tools are only aids to judgment, ways of imposing structure on complex problems. In the end, people, not tools, make the difficult decisions that create the future, exercising their best judgment in the face of uncertainties that can't be resolved. Without innovation and risk taking, there would be no economic progress. The discipline of management helps to increase the odds that the risky business of innovation will pay off.

Chapter 8

Delivering Results: First, You Focus

Results are obtained by exploiting opportunities, not by solving problems.

—Peter F. Drucker

The ability to deliver results year in and year out is one of the hallmarks of a seasoned professional. Among managers, the phrase *she or he can deliver the numbers* is high praise indeed. It speaks broadly of someone you can trust—absolutely—to meet commitments. And, more narrowly, it tells you that at the end of the day, or the quarter, or the year, there will be no surprises. The organization will *meet plan*.

Results don't just happen, nor are they primarily a function of working harder, or even working meaner. Similarly, the ability to deliver results isn't something that a few lucky people happen to be born with. It is usually learned on the job, apprentice-style. And it is teachable, because it largely rests on a handful of basic performance disciplines, which have evolved over decades of practice. These disciplines, in turn, are built on a couple of very simple principles.

The first is *Pareto's Law,* more commonly known as the *80-20 rule,* and also referred to as the *principle of imbalance.* What do the numbers 80-20 refer to? Think of them as the answer this question: "What percentage of results are produced by what percentage of causes?" Often, 80 percent of a company's sales and/or profits come from 20 percent of its customers. Or, 80 percent of its profits come from 20 percent of its products. Closer to home, 80 percent of your household expenditures probably come from 20 percent of the items in your budget. When Jack Welch describes his job as CEO of GE as putting "the best people on the biggest opportunities and the best allocation of dollars in the right places" he is affirming Pareto's Law. Applied to organizations, it means that performance will depend *disproportionately* on doing a few things really well. This is why it is critical to match an organization's resources to those activities that make a difference.

The second principle also goes under a number of names and variations. In Silicon Valley, it is called *Moore's Law,* which has to do with the speed at which computing power improves. In Japan, it's called *kaizen,* step-by-step improvement. In Detroit and other manufacturing centers, it is referred to as *continuous improvement.* These have all become important and useful management buzzwords since the 1980s. But the discipline of self-improvement has deep roots in American history, as anyone who has read even a brief excerpt from Benjamin Franklin's *Autobiography* will know. The simple idea is that you have to do better today than you did yesterday and better tomorrow than you did today. As Sam Walton put it: "You can't just keep doing what works one time, because everything around you is always changing."

Setting Priorities and the 80-20 Rule

Five weeks after Meg Whitman became CEO of eBay in 1998, she led a two-day marketing retreat to review data about eBay's users. If you know the dollar volume of transactions each seller on eBay is responsible for (which, of course, eBay did) you can easily draw up a list with two columns. The first column ranks customers in descending order from the largest dollar volume to the smallest. The second column records the cumulative value of their transactions. (If the first name in column one accounted for $50,000 and the second $40,000, the first number in column two would be $50,000, the second would be $90,000, and so on.) Now, imagine going down the second column and drawing a line at the point where the cumulative sales number represents 80 percent of eBay's total volume. Where would this line fall? How concentrated were eBay's sales?

Whitman and her team found that 20 percent of the users represented 80 percent of eBay's volume. This information wasn't just nice to know. On the contrary, it informed decisions that were critical for eBay's growth and profitability. At the time, when eBay's managers zeroed in on this crucial 20 percent to understand who these people were, they learned that most were serious collectors. So, Whitman and her team decided to pursue these customers not by signing major portal advertising deals, as other Web sites were doing, but rather by going where collectors themselves tended to go: to specialized publications like *Doll Collector* and *Mary Beth's Beanie World*, and collector trade shows.

Concentrating on these heavy users also led to eBay's PowerSellers program, designed to improve eBay's own performance by improving the performance of its major customers. The program provides perks and recognition for three classes of power sellers: bronze users, who sell $2,000 per month; silver users, who sell $10,000 per month; and gold users, who sell $25,000 per month. As long as PowerSellers earn high marks from buyers, eBay puts a special icon next to their names, and gives them extra levels of customer service. (For example, gold sellers get a twenty-four-hour customer support hotline.)

The 80-20 rule is one of the most basic disciplines of managerial thinking. In organizations, as in many aspects of life, it is universally true that some small number of x (decisions, products, customers, distribution channels—you name it) will account for a disproportionately large percentage of results. The Italian economist Vilfredo Pareto discovered the underlying principle of the 80-20 rule, the surprising imbalance between causes and results, at the end of the nineteenth century. Pareto was studying the distribution of wealth and income, when he discovered the pattern that now bears his name. Only in the past few decades, however, has it been widely adopted in management circles. Today, Pareto's Law affects the way that millions of people work, although most of those people have never heard of him.

Although it's a mistake to take the 80-20 rule literally, it is surprising how close the actual numbers often come. Of the ten leading causes of death in the U.S., for example, the top two, or 20 percent, account for 67 percent of the deaths. This kind of imbalance characterizes most cause-and-effect relationships, and it is the overriding point of Pareto's Law: In most instances, a few things matter far more than others.

Today, every well-managed organization goes through some version of the exercise we described at eBay. In 2000, the most prosperous 20 percent of Americans accounted for 60 percent of the spending on new automobiles (up from 40 percent a decade earlier). Auto makers have been monitoring this shift and designing their products accordingly—thus, the trend to bigger vehicles loaded with all sorts of expensive options like leather seats and high-end sound systems.

The fast-food industry also depends on "heavy users," the 20 percent of its patrons who account for 60 percent of visits and an even greater percentage of sales and profits. The profile of the heavy user is a single male, under age thirty, who makes more than twenty visits per month. Concerned about generating an image problem, fast-food companies don't appeal directly to these heavy users in their advertising, but they certainly focus on meeting their needs. Kentucky

Fried Chicken, for example, knowing its heavy user is an in-car diner who dislikes picking bones while driving, launched a new line of chicken sandwiches specifically designed for them. "Our heavy users were eating a ton of chicken sandwiches elsewhere," KFC's senior director of consumer insight told the *Wall Street Journal*.

An important corollary of the 80-20 principle is that averages and aggregate numbers are useless, if not misleading, because they obscure most of the decisions that are important to performance. If some customers are unprofitable, you need to know which ones. A bank or mutual fund company may make money on its average customer, for example. But this masks the fact that small-balance accounts are real money losers and high-balance accounts generate all the profits. Only by breaking down an aggregate number into its components (as eBay did with its sellers) will the numbers yield a story that's both meaningful and actionable. One reason for the spate of new service fees banks are charging is that they're performing such analyses, and setting policies to discourage small accounts, or at least make them break even.

The problem with averages and aggregate numbers is that they often hide significant differences in the component figures. If a gauge tells you that the average temperature in your three-room apartment is seventy degrees you will reasonably expect to be comfortable. What if that average consists of three different numbers? What if it is twenty degrees in the kitchen, 120 in the bedroom, and seventy in the living room? That's another story, and a different course of action is required for each room: crank up the heat, open a window, leave it alone. An average of 1000 can be one hundred data points of 1000 each; or it can be 500 at 1999 and 500 at one. In the second case, even though the average is 1000, no individual instance is even close to that number. The 80-20 rule encourages managers to tear an aggregate number apart until it tells a story. Bleary-eyed, twenty-something analysts sometimes describe this process as *torturing the data until it confesses.*

Before the 1980s, most companies thought all their customers were equally valuable. Since then, the spread of 80-20 thinking, coupled with the greater availability of data and computer-processing power, has made *disaggregating* the numbers more and more common. Choosing which customers to serve has always been a critical dimension of strategy. Today's computing power makes *customer selection* (the relevant buzzword) an increasingly fine-grained activity. Armed with data about its power users, eBay could allocate extra resources to them to keep them happy, and to encourage them to do even more business on the site. Airlines have learned to keep track of frequent fliers and offer special rewards (which are a form of resource allocation) to encourage loyalty from their most profitable customers. Banks and mutual fund companies have no trouble figuring out whether you are a customer they want to keep. If you think your bank is trying to get rid of you, you may be right.

Pareto's Law and the Quality Revolution

Over the past two decades, well-managed companies throughout the world have built the rigorous pursuit of quality into their operations. Joseph Juran's groundbreaking *Quality Control Handbook*, published in 1951, was one of the sparks that ignited this quality revolution. Juran, a Romanian-born U.S. industrial engineer, had observed that defective products adhered to Pareto's Law: A relatively small number of quality problems accounted for most of the losses related to defects. From this, he concluded that quality could be dramatically improved by applying the 80-20 principle to an organization's production processes. This revolutionary idea, ignored at first in the United States, was enthusiastically embraced in Japan, where Juran and W. Edwards Deming, another American apostle of quality, were treated like heroes. Ultimately (after U.S. and European manufacturers had been sufficiently humbled by their Japanese competitors), it doubled back to the west under such rubrics as TQM, or total quality management, and six sigma.

GE's six sigma illustrates all the elements of this discipline. It begins with the outside–in perspective, asking customers to identify specifically what they value about a product or service. GE calls these elements CTQs, which stands for critical to quality. (The more widely used generic term for these elements is *drivers*—an important piece of business jargon—as in cost drivers, quality drivers, and profitability drivers. In each case, a driver is the 20 of the 80-20, a big cause that accounts for a disproportionate share of the results.) Once the CTQs have been identified, GE managers can work their way back through all the elements of the business system to make sure that each important step in the process contributes to a consistent, error-free outcome. Where quality levels don't conform to six sigma, managers can analyze the root causes of the poor quality and, following the 80-20 principle, fix the most important ones. Working back from customer requirements and methodically fixing anything that's out of tolerance is the way the low error rates of six sigma are achieved.

Consider the web-based, direct-delivery system that GE established in partnership with Home Depot in 2000. Previously, GE had shipped appliances to Home Depot, which kept them in inventory until they were purchased. Home Depot's problem was that it wanted to offer its customers more choices, but didn't want to hold more inventory. The solution was an in-store kiosk, which allows the Home Depot sales reps to take a customer's order for any GE appliance. The order is e-mailed directly to the nearest GE warehouse, and the appliance is then shipped directly to the customer's home.

When Home Depot said that it wanted to offer this service to every customer, GE listened attentively. The new system offered a great opportunity to cement a relationship with a retailer that had become dominant in the marketplace. However, GE, the quintessentially disciplined company, didn't say *yes* right away. First, they ran the numbers.

After carefully establishing what its customers' CTQs were and assessing its own capabilities, GE discovered that it would be able to satisfy most customers, but not all. Those who lived outside a given radius of a GE warehouse couldn't be served effectively by home delivery. So, GE and Home Depot agreed *not* to serve a handful of customers in order to offer good service to all the rest. Customers who live too far away still buy their appliances the old-fashioned way: The machine goes from GE to the store to the customer.

One CTQ surprised GE. Customers said they cared about the quality of their interactions with GE's staff even more than having the appliance delivered within twenty-four hours. If the staff were courteous and professional, customers would tolerate late deliveries or even damaged products. Armed with this new, and unexpected, information, GE invested in training installers and delivery people in the soft skills of interacting with customers. Because it zeroed in on the 80-20 of value from its customers' perspective, GE could allocate its resources appropriately. Do this consistently and methodically with every dollar you spend, and you will achieve superior performance, as GE has for the past two decades.

For most people, Pareto's Law offers both good news and bad. The bad news is that as efficient as we think we are, we waste a lot of time and effort—80 percent of what we do yields a meager 20 percent of results. The good news is that there is not only room for improvement, but also a means to accomplish it. In this sense, Juran's discovery was extraordinarily good news, because it meant that quality problems with many causes could be tackled systematically and solved. It offered a discipline to improve performance.

As with all disciplines, applying the 80-20 principle is important precisely because it isn't intuitive. Our natural tendency is to assume that most problems worth solving have too many causes and that, therefore, they can't be solved. In addition, at work, as in other aspects of our lives, there's always a lot competing for our attention. It is all too easy to scatter efforts, to fight too many battles at once. We're eternally out of time, rushing from one activity to the next, as if all were equally important and productive. When people complained to Jack Welch that they were working ninety-hour weeks, he advised them to make a list of the 20 things they were doing, then look at it hard. "Ten of them have to be nonsense," he'd say, or else they're things you shouldn't be doing yourself. Pareto's Law urges us to get better results with less effort.

Delivering results requires steady focus on the 20 percent, on the things that will have the greatest impact. Disciplined managers zoom in repeatedly on the 80-20, on the big cost and profit items where improvements will really move the needle. Over time, it is the only way an organization can get an adequate return for the time its people invest.

Resource Allocation: The Hard Part Is Saying *No*

Resource allocation is one of those awful, technocratic phrases that make people's eyes glaze over. Like *value creation*, it is abstract and colorless, a phrase that's hard to put a human face on. At the same time, defining it in plain English as *matching resources to opportunities* sounds banal. The advice is so obvious—like "buy low, sell high"—that your first reaction is probably, big deal. In fact, it is a very big deal, and it's a lot easier said than done. (Remember, this was how Jack Welch summed up his job at GE.)

Part of the difficulty of matching resources to opportunities is information: You don't always know how much an opportunity is worth, much less which of hundreds of opportunities are likely to be best. Often, the information needed to make these determinations resides with project champions who are competing against one another for resources.

Even if you have perfect information, focusing an organization's resources in the right places is never as easy as it sounds. People disagree about priorities. They build empires and defend their turf. They cling to the past, to familiar territory. They hate to stop what they're doing, because it would look and feel like an admission of failure. The math of priority setting is simple. Acting on the math is hard, because putting resources *here* means you're not going to put them *there*. It means, in other words, that you will often have to say *no*, when it is always easier and far more agreeable to say *yes*. Quantification helps, sometimes enormously, to depoliticize the difficult decisions about priorities that are critical to any organization's performance, but they remain tough decisions.

For the media, the public at large and even many people inside organizations, the human face associated with resource allocation is usually the individual who has lost out: a decent person downsized from a decent job whose life will never be the same. The minute we focus on this so-called loser's face, we forget the bigger picture, which is that without disciplined resource allocation, there would be many more faces for us to contemplate. The problem is particularly painful in health care. As members of a humane and just society, we believe no one should be denied care but, at the same time, as payors, we demand cost containment and affordable health insurance. For management, this can be mission impossible.

Humana, a large healthcare company, found itself on the horns of this dilemma when it analyzed its spending and found that the sickest 10 percent of patients accounted for 80 percent of its costs. Patients with congestive heart failure (CHF)—a chronic disease that costs the nation $17 billion a year—are among the most costly. Under its CorSolutions program, Humana applies an approach to CHF called *disease management*.

It assigns nurses to follow those patients most at risk, to call them on the phone to discuss their diet or medication, and to urge them to seek care when needed, so that they avoid the kind of crisis that often results in expensive hospital stays. Nationwide, one in five patients diagnosed with CHF dies within the first year. Humana reports that CorSolutions has cut its mortality rate in half, to one in 10. That's a *real* bottom line.

Now, here's the rub. Putting more staff to work on CHF patients meant pulling resources away from other patients, resources that Humana felt weren't producing commensurate benefits. That decision was painful for the individuals who lost benefits they had come to depend on. They sued Humana and won $80 million in damages. Our point is not to take sides, but to highlight both how difficult resource-allocation decisions can be, and how critical they are to an organization's performance. Wherever there are scarce resources, you have to make tradeoffs in order to achieve results. With a clear mandate from outsiders about the value to be created and adequate funding, management can make those tradeoffs effectively. But no manager—not even Jack Welch—can perform the miracle of the loaves and fishes that society longs for.

Because resource-allocation decisions can be wrenching, even in arenas less emotionally and politically charged than health care, for many years large corporations tended to rely on formulaic approaches. If Division A accounted for 20 percent of the corporation's sales, it would get 20 percent of the resources for investment. If expenses had to be cut by 10 percent, the order would go out to impose those cuts across the board. Allocation by the numbers eliminates the politics and numbs the pain. But it also eliminates thinking and judgment, and rules out choices that could better match resources to opportunities.

Such formulaic approaches are symptomatic of bureaucracies, of organizations more focused internally on their own politics than externally on achieving results. How else to explain, for example, the fact that the share of the U.S. defense budget going to each branch of the military has not changed in decades, despite the dramatic changes that have occurred in the threats to national security and in military technology? The less an organization is pressured by outside forces to perform, the more likely it is to allocate its resources by some inward-looking logic of compromise. It will avoid rocking the boat. But, when decision making is dominated by keeping people inside happy, the organization can easily become trapped in its own inertia.

Performance-oriented companies have smarter ways to make resource-allocation decisions, as a justly famous episode in Intel's evolution illustrates. Today, Intel is the world leader in microprocessors, the chips that power computers. These high-margin products fueled Intel's extraordinary performance for fifteen years. In the early 1980s, however, Intel was primarily a manufacturer of dynamic random access memory (DRAM) chips, competing against Japanese manufacturers who were rapidly taking share from American producers.

The story of Intel's transition from a memory company to a microprocessor company is recounted in Andy Grove's fine book, *Only the Paranoid Survive*. Even before Intel's senior executives had begun to grapple with the unthinkable prospect of exiting the DRAM business, its middle managers were quietly at work making resource-allocation decisions that paved the way for the change. Short of production capacity to make semiconductors, Intel's production planners and finance people had to make decisions daily about the mix of products its plants would make. Implicitly, they were also determining what *not* to make. The planners allocated capacity to the most profitable chips (those with the highest contribution margin per wafer, to use Intel's term for the measure). On that basis, microprocessors easily beat DRAMs.

This decision may seem like the proverbial no-brainer, especially in light of what subsequently happened in the industry. Convinced of the strategic importance of DRAMs, Japanese companies overinvested in capacity, driving prices down, while simul-

taneously driving the U.S. manufacturers out of DRAMs altogether. Then, the Koreans entered the competition as well, and the
flood of low-priced chips ruined the business. As obvious as the
answer may seem today, it was far from obvious in 1985, when, as
Andy Grove puts it, "memories *were* us." DRAMs were at the
heart of Intel's identity, and it took "the sight of unrelenting red
ink before we could summon up the gumption needed to execute a
dramatic departure from our past." Fortunately for Intel, however, its middle managers had been dealing "with allocations and
numbers in an objective world," so, by the time the senior managers made the decision to exit the memory business, its production had already been substantially redirected to microprocessors.
"The Intel production schedulers shifted wafer capacity from
memories to microprocessors because the latter were more profitable," says Grove. "Meanwhile we senior managers were
trapped by the inertia of our previous success."

The Discipline of Letting Go

Pulling the plug on an existing activity can be a wrenching
experience, as Andy Grove's comments attest. It is also an essential piece of delivering results. Anyone who has managed R&D in
the pharmaceuticals industry will tell you that performance there
is a function not only of betting on the right projects, but also of
knowing when it's time to walk away from a project that isn't
turning out as you had hoped. Developing a new drug takes so
much time and money that a research project leader may work on
as few as five or six projects in an entire career. Imagine the pressure this generates to keep a project going—and how personally
devastating the company's decision to kill a program can be.

Such decisions are necessary, however, not just in R&D but
across the board. They are the only way to liberate resources from
yesterday's priorities. Always an astute observer of human behavior, Peter Drucker noted repeatedly that the greatest obstacle to

innovation in organizations is the unwillingness to let go of yesterday's success, and to free up resources that no longer contribute to results. He once referred to the products and businesses we cling to most tenaciously, despite their mediocre performance, as "investments in managerial ego." The solution, says Drucker, is the discipline of "systematic abandonment," a discipline Jack Welch applied when he undertook to remake GE in 1981. We needed "to ask ourselves Peter Drucker's very tough question, 'If you weren't already in the business, would you enter it today?'" he has said. "And if the answer is no, face that second difficult question, 'What are you going to do about it?'"

People hate to lose turf, to lose face, to lose, period. They get stuck in a mental trap that economists call *sunk costs*. A sunk cost is an investment of time or money that can no longer be recovered or put to another use. In plain English, it's money down the drain. This concept is covered early in any basic finance course, and the lesson is an important one: When you are evaluating whether to invest today, you have to ignore what you've already invested. Instead you must ask, will I get a good return on the money and time I'm going to invest from this moment forward?

This lesson has to be taught because it's not how most people are wired emotionally. Psychologists have known for years that people hate to walk away from decisions they've already made. This finding has been borne out anew by studies in the field of behavioral finance, which focuses on the psychology of investing. It makes little difference whether the mistake involves buying a stock, or developing a new product or hiring an employee: People much prefer to carry on in the hopes that their earlier decisions will be vindicated. The discipline of sunk costs helps managers avoid this trap, and can deter them from throwing good money after bad.

As the pace of competition has quickened, businesses must be more disciplined than ever about letting go, or they will squander the resources they need to build for tomorrow. In the public sector, this challenge is equally pressing, and even harder to deal with. Government has few natural mechanisms to shut programs down once they've been started, so they—and the spending associated with them—often take on a life of their own. Similarly, in nonprofits, it's terribly easy for people to get caught up in the belief that all of the organization's activities are equally good (and therefore deserve to be continued), because each somehow supports the mission. In practice, some activities will always be more effective and productive than others. But absent the external discipline of the capital markets and the means to match revenues with costs, nonprofits have little incentive to face up to hard choices among competing priorities. So unless a social enterprise imposes the discipline of letting go on itself, it is unlikely to redirect critical resources to the most productive uses.

Beating Yesterday

In the mid-1960s, when the computer revolution was just getting underway, Intel's legendary co-founder Gordon Moore prophesied that chip capacity would double every eighteenth months. This prophecy came to be known as Moore's Law—and it became sacred writ in Silicon Valley. Used by extension to talk about the incredible pace of continuous improvement that technology delivers, the phrase sounds like a law of physics. It's not. It's really a business objective, a goal set and subscribed to by Intel's managers and engineers.

Stripped of the reference to computer chips, Moore's Law reflects an attitude toward self-improvement that has existed for a very long time. The annals of business history are filled with people who just couldn't leave well enough alone. You see it in the dogged persistence of Taylor's scientific management, with its underlying faith that you could keep on making work more efficient. It is equally apparent in the restless spirit and constant tinkering of men like Henry Ford and George Eastman. During the past twenty years, however, what once seemed like a quaint and admirable habit among an industrious minority has turned into something more like a mass obsession bordering on hysteria. Andy Grove, Gordon Moore's successor at Intel, created the catch phrase for this obsession: "Only the paranoid survive" (sometimes referred to as *Grove's Corollary*).

Long before benchmarking and best practices had become management buzzwords, however, Sam Walton had all his store managers filling out "Beat Yesterday" ledgers, simple forms that tracked daily sales in comparison to same-day sales one year earlier. These ledgers would be right at home alongside Ben Franklin's childhood diaries. Comparing today's performance to yesterday's gave Wal*Mart's managers a powerful stimulus to raise the bar and institutionalize continuous improvement in their operations.

Walton described what he was trying to accomplish this way: "We were really trying from the beginning to become the very best operators—the most professional managers—that we could. There's no question that I have the personality of a promoter. . . . But underneath that personality, I have always had the soul of an operator, someone who wants to make things work well, then better, then the best they possibly can." Walton institutionalized this spirit through a host of mechanisms that encouraged employees to come up with new ideas and put them to work. The "store within a store" organization he developed, for example, gave managers the autonomy to innovate within their departments.

Whenever an experiment with a new way to cut costs or enhance service was successful, it was rolled out to all the other stores. Wal*Mart's signature "people greeters," associates who welcome shoppers as they enter the store, were the result of a successful experiment in Crowley, Louisiana to reduce *shrinkage,* the industry's term for shoplifting. The fact that most people perceive the greeters as a service extra—and not as a way to reduce costs—makes the idea even better.

What Walton did as a matter of instinct three or four decades ago, managers now practice more systematically under the banner of benchmarking and best practices. These related disciplines are keeping more and more organizations marching to the steady drumbeat of continuous improvement. The idea is to compare the performance of your products or processes with those that are best in class, even if this means going outside your organization or industry. The goal is to discover who does something best (whether it's processing an order, for example, or running a distribution center), and learn from their practice how to improve yours. Benchmarking became widespread in the 1980s, as a result of heightened competition and the need to improve productivity and quality. Today it is widely embraced as a way of bringing new ideas into a company, as well as maintaining a pace of continuous improvement.

The effects of these disciplines are evident in the fast-food industry. In fact, Ray Kroc, McDonald's founder, got his insight about creating value as the result of what today would be called best-practice thinking. Remember, Kroc was a veteran milk-shake machine salesman, who was curious to know why the McDonald brothers were buying eight milk-shake machines when the typical restaurant only needed one or two. When Kroc went to see for himself in 1954, he was amazed. With a stripped-down menu and lightning-fast service, the McDonald brothers had brought efficiency to the food business. Kroc, who had seen the operations of hundreds of restaurants, recognized a best practice when he saw it. What was to become an enormous global industry was born.

In the 1970s, Wendy's founder, Dave Thomas, made the drive-through window a staple of his chain, realizing its potential to boost sales without using up dining room space or requiring extra labor. It soon became clear that Wendy's enjoyed higher profit margins than its competitors, and the idea began to spread. Originally, the drive-through window was something of an afterthought. Today, it has become the main event, accounting for almost 65 percent of fast-food revenue, and growing faster than on-premises sales. For this reason, product development resources are aimed at creating new menu items that can easily be consumed in cars, such as salads packed in containers that fit in cup-holders.

The industry's search for best practice is focused on speed, not (as is the case with Dell Computer) because it translates into lower costs, but because speed itself is what its customers value. This is especially true for the drive-through customer. According to McDonald's CEO Jack Greenberg, for every six seconds saved at the drive-through, sales increase by 1 percent. So not surprisingly, everyone is now measuring drive-through speed and using the latest computing and sensing technology to make it faster. McDonald's, for example, wants to shave time by allowing drivers to bypass the cash window, so it's experimenting with the same windshield transponders that automatically pay highway tolls. The Wendy's in Darien, Connecticut, which is set up as a best-practice model that other Wendy's managers can come to visit, is a high-tech wonder. Timers with underground sensors placed at various points in the drive-through lane measure nearly every aspect of the store's performance, beeping to indicate the location of a problem if an order isn't filled fast enough. At last count, Darien's drive-through time was less than two minutes, beating the chain's average of two minutes and thirty seconds—and we guarantee that by the time you read this, it will be even faster.

As Wendy's and McDonald's illustrate, the *fast* in fast food doesn't happen by itself. Companies find the right measures of performance. They track them. And they work systematically to improve them, all the while dreaming up new solutions, and testing them to see if they work.

Saving a few seconds of the time it takes to deliver an order of

French fries may seem trivial, but what about saving lives? The discipline of best practice can be put to noble uses as well. In 1994, Dr. Kim Bateman of Intermountain Health Care in Utah set out to identify the best practice for treating community-acquired pneumonia, a simple lung infection, that is one of the nation's leading killers. Bateman was stunned by what he found. There were no standard practices within the system. Studying 101 patient cases, Bateman found they were treated with sixty-eight different combinations of antibiotics. Yet the study also showed that in nearly all cases one protocol would have been best. IHC has now adopted this protocol, and Bateman estimates that it may save as many as fifty lives each year in the IHC system.

Similarly, the Northern New England Collaborative, a hospital consortium, has achieved one of the lowest coronary-bypass death rates in the country. This successful outcome began with a study that showed significant disparities among the mortality rates in the region's hospitals. Instead of burying the results of this study (which many doctors refused to believe were true), the members of the Collaborative decided to share information with one another about their practices and outcomes.

In a PBS documentary, Bill Nugent, the chief cardiac surgeon at the Dartmouth-Hitchcock Medical Center in New Hampshire, recalled his first reaction to the data—"terror." He described the fear of exposure and the helpless feeling of not knowing what to do about the problems. Before long, however, he and his colleagues in the Collaborative identified and adopted a series of best practices, ranging from how patients are worked up before surgery to how blood is transfused during the operation to how the handoff from the operating room to the intensive care unit is managed. Together these changes produced a 24 percent reduction in the hospitals' mortality rate. Best practices prevent one in four deaths.

Interest in best practices that can improve care as well as manage costs is spreading throughout the medical community. Minnesota has long been one of the pioneers in developing managed care. In 2001, the state took another giant step forward, when its five leading health insurers announced that they would endorse a set of guidelines for treating fifty common ailments. The guidelines, or protocols, were developed by physicians at hospitals and medical centers throughout the state, and will be updated continuously as new medicines and procedures become available.

This is how the discipline of management delivers results—and it recaps the major ideas we've been tracking in the preceding chapters as well as this one. You need numbers to tell you where you stand, but performance isn't a matter of numbers alone. It is what people do with the numbers that counts. They must trust others enough to get past their own defensiveness. They must have not only the courage to face reality, but the curiosity to ask why things are as they are, and the openness to search for innovative practice wherever it is to be found. All of this is essential to delivering results. None of it happens without trust, without the social context of values, which is the subject of our next chapter.

Chapter 9

Managing People: Which Values Matter and Why

Somebody once said that in looking for people to hire, you look for three qualities: integrity, intelligence, and energy. And if they don't have the first, the other two will kill you. You think about it; it's true. If you hire somebody without [integrity], you really want them to be dumb and lazy.

—Warren Buffett

In holding the subject of people until the last chapter, we could argue that we were saving the best for last. More to the point, however, we've been talking about nothing *but* people from the very start—beginning with the human purpose that animates organizations in the first place, then working through the ways management has learned to transform that purpose into performance. All the disciplines we've discussed—from creating a common reality to allocating resources—help transform the specialized contributions of individuals into the joint performance of organizations.

Students of management and their professors tend to divide the world into two separate domains: numbers and people. There are the "hard" subjects like finance and operations, and the "soft" ones like leadership and organizational behavior. This split is reinforced by histories of management thinking that trace the descendants of Taylor's scientific management on the one hand, and the social relations school on the other, as if these were competing theories.

Only in the classroom does the distinction make much sense. All good executives know that the central challenge of management is seamlessly integrating the two into a working whole. Organizations are economic machines, and they are also social systems. Machines do what they're told, day in and day out. They don't have to like what they do, or believe in it, or care about it. They don't withhold their best efforts when they feel unappreciated. Nor, on the other hand, do machines accomplish miracles when they're inspired. Social systems are more complicated, as are the individuals who constitute them.

This has always been frustrating to those managers who prize control above all else. Henry Ford, who took command and control to a pathological extreme, thought he could do all the thinking himself for his company. "Why is it that whenever I ask for a pair of hands," he reportedly complained, "a brain comes attached?" Peter Drucker had the last word. One can never simply hire a hand, he wrote. The whole person always comes with it.

And that's the problem. The whole person, without whom nothing would get done, often makes it hard to get anything done. Caught in our own egos, we are forever getting in our own and one another's way. Equally problematic, most people are deeply— and rightly—resistant to being *managed*. In fact, the real insight about managing people is that, ultimately, you don't. The best performers are people who know enough and care enough to manage themselves. This chapter is about what that means for everyone, managers and nonmanagers alike. It is about management's responsibility to provide a context of values within which individuals can manage themselves, and it is about what it means for individuals to take responsibility for their own performance.

Back when labor was mostly a matter of brawn, the work itself could be managed: analyzed, organized, and specified. Workers had only to do exactly what they were told, and supervisors made sure they complied. But even as the supervisory component of management has shrunk considerably, we continue to confuse authority and control. Having the authority to reward and punish—being in charge—isn't the same thing as being able to control an individual's performance. When people become managers for the first time, they often experience a rude awakening. At last they take control, only to find they've been taken hostage instead. They realize that they are now dependent as never before, because management creates performance *through* others. Without the willing cooperation of others, management can accomplish very little.

This has always been true to some extent, but it is especially true in modern economies, where there is a sizable knowledge or service component in most jobs. The most powerful sources of value are locked in people's heads, and in their hearts. You can't supervise an engineer into writing better software code, nor can you command a nurse to care about her patients. For knowledge workers, who, by definition, know more about their jobs than their bosses do, supervision is a very special kind of hell. The same is true for *emotional labor,* a phrase coined by the sociologist Arlie Hochschild to describe work whose performance depends on people being nicer than is natural, like flight attendants, or nastier, like bill collectors. (Hochschild's 1983 book is aptly titled *The Managed Heart.*)

This creates a profound challenge for management. On the one hand, performance depends on the contributions of individuals, each of whom is just that, stubbornly individual, each of whom needs to feel valued. On the other hand, while individuals—and especially the right ones—are fundamental, the organization and its purpose comes first. Performance depends on collaboration, on teamwork, on individuals committing their talent and their best effort to something larger than themselves. Resolving this tension between the individual and the organization is at the heart of management's work. Increasingly, this is being done through values: the shared values that tell individuals in an organization what's worth striving for, the basic trust that liberates them to strive, and the respect for individuals that acknowledges their unique contributions to the whole.

Managing Culture: The Social Dimension

In 1992, GE's top executives were attending an off-site meeting in Boca Raton, Florida. It had been a great year, and the mood was celebratory. Then, Jack Welch spoke. "Look around you: There are five fewer officers here than there were last year. One was fired for the numbers, four were fired for values."

Welch went on to elaborate, dividing his managers into four distinct types. Type I, he said, is "everybody's star. These people deliver on commitments, financial or otherwise, and share our values." Type IIs are the opposite: "They do not meet commitments, nor share our values—nor last long at GE." Type IIIs try hard, miss some commitments, but work well with people and share the values. They deserve another chance. Type IVs deliver the numbers, but do so by forcing them out of people. Says Welch, "This is your big shot, your tyrant, the person you'd love to be rid of— but oh those numbers." Looking back, in his 1997 Letter to Shareholders, Welch wrote, "The decision to begin removing Type IVs was a watershed . . . but it had to be done if we wanted GE people to be open, to speak up, to share."

What values was Welch talking about? They were love of speed, hatred of bureaucracy, excitement about change—the values GE holds dear. These are neither universal ethical principles nor absolute moral values. They are the shared beliefs that constitute this particular organization's culture—its set of assumptions about how we do things and who we are. An organization's values, unlike ethics, are matters of deep belief about which honest people can disagree. The question isn't whether one company's values are better than another's, but which are better-suited to helping the organization achieve its purpose. The real measure is fit.

Consider Southwest Airlines. With its incredible record of growth and profitability, Southwest has been the big success story of the airline industry over the past three decades. From the very start, its strategy has been different. Most carriers will get you from any point A to any point B, using major airports, offering meals and assigned seats, usually requiring that you change planes along the way. Southwest offers something different. By focusing on some routes—but not all—and by stressing no-frills, point-to-point, short-haul travel between less congested airports, Southwest can fly you there for less. Because it doesn't try to be all things to all passengers, Southwest's costs are lower than most other airlines. Like Dell and Wal*Mart, then, it can charge lower prices and still be profitable. Being low cost is essential to Southwest's success. That's strategy.

Now, execution. Southwest's cost advantage depends on more than its focused product offering. It also depends on its workforce of highly motivated, highly productive people. Southwest is heavily unionized, but there are no confining work rules to prevent people from pitching in when there's a job to be done. As a result, labor costs are lower, and planes are in service carrying paying passengers more of the time. Gate turnaround time—the elapsed time between a plane's arrival at the gate and its next departure—is often cited as an example of Southwest's cost advantage through people. A Southwest ground crew of six routinely takes fifteen minutes to do what other airlines do in thirty-five minutes with a crew of twelve.

Southwest differentiates itself on service, as well as on price. Consistent with its low-cost strategy, Southwest defines service as treating customers with warmth and friendliness, not as providing costly amenities like fine meals served on china. Herb Kelleher, Southwest's widely admired founding CEO, believes that the key to delivering such service is putting employees first. "If they're happy, satisfied, dedicated, and energetic, they'll take real good care of the customers. When the customers are happy, they come back. And that makes the shareholders happy." At Southwest, people and profits are explicitly linked, and every Southwest employee is taught why the company has achieved profits consistently for twenty-five years, a record matched by no other major airline.

Southwest's culture is responsible for keeping employees happy, satisfied, dedicated and energetic. The idea that work should be fun is one of its core values, as is the notion that every person makes a difference and should be treated with dignity and respect. Words like these trip off the tongue easily, but few companies succeed in practicing what they preach. Southwest has been different.

Southwest uses a wide range of systems and activities to reinforce its values, from training at its University for People to compensation to company-sponsored contests, parties, and celebrations. Flight attendants are encouraged, for example, to use their imagination in entertaining passengers. They are celebrated for coming up with offbeat ideas like in-flight who-has-the-biggest-hole-in-their-socks contests. We could cite dozens of individual practices, but the point isn't any one thing that Southwest does, it's the consistent whole that adds up to a culture, and the constant effort with which it is maintained.

When another airline went bankrupt, for example, a team of Southwest employees was sent to Chicago to interview the people who had lost their jobs. For most companies, this would have been a cold-blooded exercise in recruiting. For Southwest, it became an occasion to practice what they preach about treating people with dignity. A training team helped the job seekers write resumes, even those they knew they wouldn't be hiring. Southwest offered to interview everyone, and set up appointments so as not to keep people waiting. In contrast, rival United Airlines kept the same people standing in line for two hours just to fill out a job application.

"Setting an example is not the main means of influencing others," Albert Einstein is reported to have said, "it is the only means." Certainly, leaders like Sam Walton and Herb Kelleher put a personal stamp on the organizations they create, embodying the values for all to emulate. Known for his wacky sense of humor, Kelleher once arm-wrestled another CEO for rights to the slogan "Just Plane Smart." He has appeared in print ads for Southwest dressed as Elvis. Colorful leaders make good press—and fuel the notion that personalities drive cultures. However, there are plenty of charismatic people who don't leave effective organizations behind, and vice versa. Personalities come and go, but only if leaders create distinctive cultures will there be a lasting context of values to guide and motivate people.

Making Values Come Alive

Culture building is hard work. It requires communication, communication, and, then, more communication. It thrives on simple messages, repeated again and again—one of Jack Welch's special gifts. It often takes a talent for overacting, big gestures that can be seen in the back row. It also takes a flair for symbol and storytelling. We saw earlier how performance measures make an organization's mission concrete. Similarly, story, ritual, and symbol are powerful ways of making values tangible.

Values are abstract. Set in stories, they come alive, and the stories become parables for right action. Stories are not only easy to remember, but they have the power to inspire, offering ordinary people the chance to become heroes. One of the most famous stories involves Nordstrom's long-standing policy to accept cheerfully any merchandise returned by customers, with or without proof of purchase. The hero of this story, told and retold to trainees, is the salesperson who accepted a badly used set of tires, a product Nordstrom doesn't carry. By its very outrageousness, the story establishes a principle everyone can understand. Nordstrom is committed to customer satisfaction. This, the story says, is how far we'll go to satisfy a customer.

Other companies tell different sorts of stories, tailored to their missions and strategies. At 3M, for example, the stories celebrate innovation. There's the story about the scientist who sang in the choir and wished his bookmark wouldn't fall out of the hymnal. That's the story of Post-it Notes, the ubiquitous yellow stickies. At Southwest, the stories focus on heroic individual initiatives in the service of passengers, like the gate agent whose quick thinking and big heart saved a passenger's vacation. The traveler, unaware that pets aren't allowed to accompany their owners, shows up for his flight with his dog in tow. Rather than see the customer's vacation ruined, the gate agent takes care of the dog for two weeks while the customer is away.

City Year, the nonprofit that brings young volunteers together for a year of community service, faces a peculiar challenge in instilling its values and creating a cohesive culture. By design, City Year's workforce turns over every year, so the organization must be re-created constantly. Also by design, its corps of volunteers is diverse in education, economic background, and race. Teaching kids to be citizens in a diverse society is, in fact, City Year's mission.

City Year's purpose is to create citizens, not soldiers, but it has learned from the military how to use symbols and rituals to create instant bonding. City Year assigns the kids to teams of ten to twelve members, and initiates them into a strong culture that emphasizes "one corps," teamwork, and leadership. City Year's culture borrows the best from others: the esprit de corps of an elite military unit, the accountability of business, the urgency of a tight political campaign, and the mutual regard of a family.

At City Year, both discipline and energy are core values, essential to the organization's theory of change. These are symbolized by City Year's bright uniforms and by their morning ritual of calisthenics. City Year's idealism is captured in a store of inspirational stories, and a shared vocabulary, which creates a sense of group identity. Members, for example, are encouraged to "moccasin" their ideas, alluding to a Native-American prayer, "Grant that I not criticize my brother until I have walked a mile in his moccasins."

Values expressed through culture convey the message of a common purpose to which it is worth devoting one's energies. Such values have enormous motivating power. Historically, organizations have relied more heavily on work rules and financial incentives, and these will never go away entirely. People need clarity about roles, authority, and accountability. They must also be paid appropriately for their efforts. To describe these requirements as "basic hygiene" isn't to assume that every organization gets them right.

But the productivity of knowledge and service work poses additional challenges. How could you possibly handle—through structure, or procedures, or financial incentives alone—the kind of behavior captured in the story of Southwest's gate agent and the passenger's dog? Yet, increasingly, in modern economies that's what performance is all about.

At Southwest, values are far more important than rules. Around 1990, the company decided to throw out its three-hundred-page corporate handbook, and to rename its human resources function the People Department. Ann Rhoades, then head of HR, was concerned that her department would become what it is in many organizations, a policing function. To reinforce the message, Colleen Barrett, Southwest's president and chief operating officer, created this plain-English statement of policy: "No employee will ever be punished for using good judgment and good old common sense when trying to accommodate a Customer—no matter what our other rules are."

Management's Golden Rule: Trust

We're taught, as children, to follow the Golden Rule, to do unto others as we would have them do unto us. The unspoken corollary is to treat others with kindness and respect. If management had its own golden rule, it would be this: Trust others as you would have them trust you. There would also be this corollary: Deliver what you promise.

There's an economic explanation for this. Increasingly, economics has become a quantitative discipline, one of the "numbers" subjects. But its underlying aim has always been to explain human behavior. Its eighteenth century pioneers, like Adam Smith, studied ethics and moral philosophy. Of all the nations in Europe, Smith wrote, "the Dutch, the most commercial, are the most faithful to their word." This isn't a case of national character, Smith explained. It's self-interest: "When people seldom deal with one another, we find that they are somewhat disposed to cheat, because they can gain more by a smart trick than they can lose by the injury which it does to their character." When we worry today about being scammed by some anonymous merchant on the Internet, or the guy on the street corner peddling phony Rolex watches out of a cardboard suitcase, we are reaffirming the enduring truth of Adam Smith's observation.

Modern behavioral economists extend the explanation beyond self-interest. Matthew Rabin, winner of the prestigious John Bates Clark Medal in 2001, has demonstrated that people respond to fairness and reciprocity. They behave toward others as they perceive others to be behaving toward them even if such behavior does not maximize income or well-being.

Reputation matters in business, whether it's the reputation of a company, a brand, or an individual, and reputations are built on integrity. Are you who you seem? Can you be counted on to keep your word? What was true about reputation in Adam Smith's mercantile economy is even more true today. Because information moves faster and is far more difficult to contain, reputations can be tarnished more quickly. As a result, observes Scott McNealy, CEO of Sun Microsystems, trust is more valuable than ever before. "Promises," he says, "are still only promises until somebody delivers the goods. That's still what reputations are based on. . . . In business, as in life, character matters. It is real. So is integrity; it may be intangible (it can even be faked, for a time), but that doesn't make it any less real."

Organizations—and individuals—that say one thing and do another may be able to fake it for a while, but they are unlikely to achieve greatness. If management is not trustworthy, employees will neither share their best ideas nor give their all. Without trust, an organization won't be credible to its own members, nor will individuals be credible to their colleagues. When people are unwilling to extend trust to each other, teamwork and collaboration fall apart. Without trust, in other words, performance grinds to a halt.

Breakdowns of trust take many forms. In the summer of 2000, the Communications Workers of America staged an eighteen-day strike against the phone company Verizon. One of the principal issues was stress, and one of the principal causes of stress was a Verizon rule that its service agents follow, word for word, a scripted message. Every call had to end with the phrase, "Did I provide you with outstanding service today?" Verizon's rule sent a message to its employees: We don't trust you to think and react appropriately on your own.

The problem with scripts, said one union official and a longtime service rep, is that they "don't sound natural." They make the speaker sound insincere. And worse, as one agent put it, they leave you feeling like "a total idiot." That's precisely how she felt after she had managed to win over an irate customer. "You're the nicest rep I ever had," the caller said, despite his previous bad encounters with the company. The agent wanted to say a simple thank-you and goodbye. She knew, however, that a supervisor might be listening in on the call. So, reluctantly, and against her better judgment, she read the scripted message, which immediately set the customer off again.

To make matters worse, Verizon workers had the script in one hand, and the company's values statement in the other. The company proclaims its values to be integrity, respect, imagination, passion, and service. The clash between the words on the page and the company's behavior wasn't lost on its employees. Verizon said publicly that its values statement was inspired by the book, *Built to Last*, a deservedly influential study of what makes great companies great. Unfortunately, Verizon missed the key point about values, which authors Jim Collins and Jerry Porras make: Above all, the core values that animate a company must be authentic.

People outside the organization may not like those values—as many people, for example, dislike the values of the cigarette-maker Phillip Morris or of the National Rifle Association. But if those values reflect what people in that organization really care about, and if they fit the business model and the strategy, those values will contribute to performance by giving guidance and inspiration to the people inside the company. They will help people select the organizations in which they are most likely to feel at home, in which their own energies will mesh with the organization's purposes. That's why great organizations often have a cult-like quality. They can be extraordinary places to work . . . if you fit. If you don't, as Jack Welch said, you probably won't last long.

In contrast, mediocre organizations create inauthentic "communities," in which people know they have to pay lip service to values nobody really believes or lives by. It's a cynical game. There are only survivors, no real winners. This source of stress in the modern workplace is a favorite subject of Dilbert cartoonist Scott Adams. Although it may help to laugh about it, most people yearn for organizations worthy of their loyalty and trust.

Respect for the Individual

No value is more universally and loudly proclaimed in organizations than respect for the individual. Like the phrases *value creation* and *thinking outside the box,* this one, too, often makes people cringe because it is so often said insincerely. Nevertheless, like trust, it's genuinely fundamental to management because it's essential to performance. Management may create the context that makes performance possible, but it is individuals who perform. Just as democracy is built on the proposition that all people are created equal, so management—effective management, that is—is built on respect for the individual. The fact that these values are often violated doesn't make them less important.

What does respect for the individual mean, and how is it translated into management practice? First, it means accepting that each person is different, and therefore good at different things. We come with different gifts, talents, attitudes, ways of thinking. What matters most to performance is getting the right individual for the job. Management's role is to spot talent, and to put it where it can contribute to performance. In practice, then, hiring the right people is one of management's most critical responsibilities.

This is a very old idea. Hiring the right person for the job was one of the core principles of scientific management laid out by Frederick Winslow Taylor a century ago. When he studied seventy-five pig-iron handlers at Bethlehem Steel, he found that only one in eight was physically right for the job. Working at a bicycle ball-bearing plant, Taylor came up with a number of productivity-enhancing ideas, but the most important of all, he said, was selecting the "right girls," in this case, those with quick reflexes.

Hiring the right people, then figuring out where to put them is the human dimension of resource allocation or, as Jack Welch described his role, "putting the best people on the biggest opportunities." In order to do that job effectively, Welch made a point of getting to know every one of GE's 500 top managers, and personally signed off on their promotions. He also interviewed anyone who was hired from the outside for one of those 500 jobs. Look at any organization known for its ability to execute and you will find a robust process for hiring, promoting, and firing people.

Southwest Airlines is a case in point. As of the late 1990s, Southwest screened about 200,000 applicants per year, interviewed 35,000, and hired 4,000. The interviews are done not by human-resource professionals, but by peers; that is, pilots hire pilots, baggage handlers hire baggage handlers. The company's emphasis on fun doesn't mean it isn't highly disciplined. It has taken a best-practices approach to defining the kind of talent the company needs. The People Department identified the top thirty-five pilots, for example, then interviewed them to identify traits that the thirty-five shared. Team skills turned out to be important, so Southwest probes candidates for concrete examples of their team-work, and listens for warning signs like candidates who say "I" all the time. Southwest turned down a pilot with outstanding flying credentials because he was rude to a Southwest receptionist during the recruiting process.

More than anything else, says Herb Kelleher, "We draft great attitudes. If you don't have a good attitude we don't want you, no matter how skilled you are. We can change skill levels through training. We can't change attitude." *Attitude* refers to Southwest's values, to the sense of fun and the respect for people that South-west holds dear. These values reinforce teamwork, which matters not because it's the latest management fad, but because it keeps

Southwest's costs down and fosters the esprit that's part of the customer experience. That's what Southwest means by a "great attitude," and why it's essential to the company's performance.

Kelleher, and all good managers, understand that each person is different. And good managers have the wisdom to distinguish what is teachable and what isn't. A manager can help people discover their strengths, and help people to get better at what they're good at, but a manager can't and shouldn't change who a person is. In most organizations, too little time is spent on hiring the right people and understanding their talent, while far too much time and energy is wasted trying to fix unfixable weaknesses.

Like many important, basic management disciplines, this *is* the conventional wisdom. It's just not the conventional practice. Enduring truths like this are periodically rediscovered and presented as radical new insights. But the real insight here is a humbling one about the difficulty of the task. If these were easy and natural things to do, we'd all just do them.

Similarly, we would all accept more gracefully and less critically management's need to fire people who are in jobs where they can't perform. When it comes to people, the failure to "let go" always impairs execution. Delay is bad for the organization as a whole and, perhaps, even worse for the individual in question. It means he's in the wrong place, a place where he'll never succeed. Despite the care Southwest takes in selecting people, they know they won't get it right every time. That's why, says Colleen Barrett, "we've got to be pretty darn religious watching that person's performance during the probationary period. That sounds strange for a family-oriented company, but if we see a misfit with teamwork or an attitude, we will counsel once or twice and we will be harsh."

Waiting too long to act when individuals aren't right for the job is a pervasive problem—in all organizations and at all levels of an organization—but it poses an especially vexing problem for nonprofit organizations, which have to manage without the discipline of the bottom line. In such an environment, underperformance has no consequences, or so it can seem. Quarterly earnings don't take a hit, the stock price doesn't fall. But the organization's ability to achieve its mission is impaired, and that is a serious consequence. When William Bratton transformed the New York City Police Department in the mid-1990s, he not only created new systems to focus the force on results; he replaced 75 percent of the precinct commanders.

Operating without the discipline of customers and capital markets—the outsiders who will let you know quickly when your performance doesn't measure up—nonprofits often rely on their boards to play that role. One of the board's responsibilities is to hold individuals accountable for their performance. In practice, however, they rarely do. The executive director of an arts organization described it this way. "For twenty years I have carefully selected smart businesspeople for my board. But they seem to check everything they know about accountability at the door. They tolerate behavior and performance in my organization that they'd never put up with in their own companies. In fact, they're so intent on being noble and being nice, they don't think about performance at all."

An organization can have the noblest mission and the best strategy in the world but, without the right people, it will never succeed at execution. Given the importance of hiring and firing, the subject gets relatively little attention in management education. Perhaps that's because the most valuable lessons are emotional ones which are hard to convey in the classroom. One Harvard Business School class became a word-of-mouth legend many years ago because it tackled the subject in an unusual way. Some eighty-five first-year students, sectionmates who go through the entire first year together, were debating with characteristic vigor the options open to the manager-protagonist of the day's case. The students sit in semicircular rows in an amphitheater-like setting. The professor in the pit this day was himself something of a legend for toughness.

"What would you do?" the professor asks.

A student volunteers. "Fire him."

Silence. Then, looking the young man in the eye, the professor says:

"I'd like you to leave my class. Pick up your books and get out of here."

"What?" the student asks, visibly confused.

"Get out. You're no longer part of my class. I don't want to see you again. Just get out of here."

There was an uncomfortable silence in the room. The student gathered his belongings and began to make his way up the aisle toward the exit.

"Come back and sit down. Now you know what it feels like to be fired."

More than anything else, this is a lesson in empathy, which is probably the most important lesson a manager can learn. Empathy is yet another instance of the outside–in perspective, of seeing the world through other people's eyes. Working effectively with other people means accepting the limits of your own authority and of your own perspective. Value creation begins with seeing the world through customers' eyes. Good strategists see the world through competitors' eyes. Good negotiators see the deal through the other party's eyes. Increasingly, our working relations—up, down, and lateral—have come to resemble negotiations. It takes more than listening. It takes a willingness to enter imaginatively into someone else's world, and it's an essential dimension of treating individuals with respect.

Managing Ourselves: Looking from the Inside Out

Management, then, does a number of things that make it possible for people to manage themselves. Creating a culture whose values are aligned with the organization's purpose is an important part of it. Selecting the right individuals and encouraging them to develop their strengths is another. In addition, good managers help people manage themselves by teaching them, often by example, to think about what they are good (and bad) at, how they work and learn, what they value, what motivates them: In other words, they foster self-knowledge.

"Know thyself" was, for the ancient Greeks, the foundation of a good life and the work of a lifetime. It is indeed hard, slow work, and companies often are tempted to take shortcuts. They hire consultants who come armed with questionnaires and other so-called instruments that promise instant self-knowledge.

Michael Lewis describes one such intervention that took place at Silicon Graphics in the mid-1980s. The company's then-new CEO, Ed McCracken, was trying to control a group of contentious engineers whose ideas and values differed from his own. He could simply have confronted them. Instead, he hired a corporate psychologist to conduct a three-day off-site retreat. Each engineer filled out a questionnaire, which the psychologist turned into a graphic depiction of each one's personality. Then, one by one, each person had to sit in front of the group on a little chair, holding up his shape to scrutiny. The psychologist said that this was just a way for people to get to know each other, and kept insisting "that there were no bad people and no bad shapes. . . . It was just a shape." Then, one of the engineers held his paper up and "the shrink almost gasps. He says, 'Wow! that's perfect.'" Apparently there were right and wrong answers to the personality test after all.

This is both a misuse of psychology and an abuse of power. There's a fine line between management and manipulation. It may be hard to define in the abstract where that line falls, but people know when it's been crossed. They know when psychology is used properly as an aid to self-awareness, and when it's abused as an instrument of control.

Used wisely, tools can help. By definition, however, self-knowledge is something we all have to come to ourselves. Knowing that managers can't really manage us, we need to take responsibility for our own performance. Knowing that we're different, and that performance arises from our differences, we have to accept that the price of responsibility is self-awareness. On this score, we're all in the same boat, managers and nonmanagers alike.

Feedback helps. Again, the practice is an old one. At Bethlehem Steel, one of Taylor's innovations, a century ago, was a system to give performance feedback, "dealing with every workman as a separate individual." If a workman failed to do his task, Taylor wrote, "some competent teacher should be sent to show him exactly how his work can best be done, to guide, help, and encourage him."

Feedback and coaching of this sort ought to be easy, although it's extraordinary how little of it is actually done. Feedback is hard, whether you're on the giving or receiving end. The neutral term *feedback* belies the fact that most of us experience it as criticism, even when it comes to work practices that would seem to be highly impersonal. That, in turn, discourages even the best-intentioned coach from wanting to give feedback a second time. Breaking this cycle, and taking a basic step toward the self-awareness that allows us to make good choices about our lives, means learning to be less defensive—or, at least, learning how to prevent our defensiveness from showing.

Today, we all need to think through who we are and what we do best. That kind of self-examination takes considerable discipline, and the process is rarely painless. Most people have many more choices to make about their lives than did their grandparents and, for many of us, work is both highly specialized and an important part of our identity. As a result, the burden of understanding not only how we contribute, but where we want to contribute, lies squarely on our own shoulders.

In managing ourselves, the questions to ask are the basic questions of management. Purpose comes first. Why do I work? Is it to make money? To make a difference? To make a life? Where and how does work fit into the larger scheme of my life? (It may be a bit of a stretch, but think of it as the personal analogue to the business model, the coherent story you'd like to tell about who you are.)

As individuals we're slow to apply the principles of value creation to our own efforts. We persist in defining our performance by how hard we work at something, rather than by the results we achieve. Nothing is tougher than to break that old mindset. Until we do, we'll have trouble thinking strategically about what makes us different, what we do well and under what circumstances we do our best work. Answers to these questions are the only enduring basis for performance, and no organization has as big a stake in figuring out who we are and how we perform as we do ourselves. Some people will be better off on their own, as free agents. Most people will need to "hire" the right organization—the one whose values match their own, and whose approach to value creation can turn what makes them special into performance. And because the quality of managers varies enormously, we need to be especially careful about "hiring" the right boss.

When we described management's role at the beginning of this book, we noted a paradox of the modern economy. The more highly educated and specialized we become and, therefore, the more likely we are to work as individual contributors and to think of ourselves as free agents or independent professionals, the more we need other people to perform. We think we live in worlds of our own and can contribute as individuals; but this is only possible because some form of organization makes the specialized work we do productive.

Here then, is another paradox: The more we need to work through others, the better we need to understand ourselves.

Epilogue
Next Steps

Management discussions never end with conclusions. They end with *next steps*, because the work never stops, and whatever is learned today triggers decisions and efforts to learn more. What, then, comes next?

First, ask how your own organization—or any organization you care about—is doing.

Management's business, we said at the start, is building organizations that work. Underneath all the theory and the tools lies a commitment to performance that has powerfully altered our economy and our lives. If this book has done its job, the abstract language of management, and the words that sometimes conceal more than they reveal, will have come into sharper focus, enabling you to see *management* as distinct from individual *managers*. Because the individuals tend to take up most of the canvas, the underlying discipline is often invisible. Yet that discipline is the best yardstick you can use to determine whether an organization is measuring up to its potential, or where it may be falling short.

We began the book by saying what management isn't. It isn't supervising other people, it isn't applied economics, it isn't about occupying a privileged rung in a hierarchy, and it isn't confined to commercial enterprises.

Because we have been defining terms as we've gone along, we can now venture to say what management is.

Management is the discipline that makes joint performance possible.

Its mission is value creation, where value is defined from the outside in, by customers and owners in the case of a business; by society, more broadly, in the case of government agencies and nonprofits.

Purpose comes first. Management starts with a mission worth accomplishing, with the value it sets out to create. Management's growing ability to turn complexity and specialization into performance has made it possible to undertake missions whose variety is limited only by our capacity to imagine them, from mapping the human genome, to ending illiteracy, to producing crunchier french fries. The common element, the basis of all performance, is clarity of purpose. The first test of management is this: Does it have a clear sense of what it seeks to accomplish and has it effectively communicated that purpose to everyone in the organization?

A design to match the purpose. The second test of management is whether it can articulate a theory of how the organization will accomplish its purpose. Every successful business rests on an insight about value, and every effective nonprofit is built on a theory of change. Capturing those insights within a coherent system, a working whole, is what a good business model does. Going a critical step further, a strategy accounts for the realities of the competitive landscape—it specifies how the organization will do better by being different. Designing the organization—drawing its boundaries and lines of authority—creates the vehicle for carrying out the strategy. The second test of management, then, is this: Does its design for the enterprise fit not only its purpose, but also the external realities of competition, and the internal realities of its own capabilities and what it will take to deliver value?

The work of execution. There's an old feminist joke about the dancer Fred Astaire and his talented, but less celebrated, partner, Ginger Rogers. Fred got far more acclaim than Ginger, yet she did everything Fred did, only backwards and in high heels. Execution may always find itself in Ginger's shoes, getting less attention, perhaps, than it deserves. Strategy will always make a more gripping story. Nevertheless, management's third and ultimate test is this: Does it deliver the results it has promised? Execution lies in setting goals and tracking measures of progress, in innovating to balance today's performance with tomorrow's, in setting priorities and allocating resources to them, in delegating responsibility and holding people accountable, and in energizing and inspiring people to manage themselves in pursuit of the common mission. If management doesn't do all these things well, it will not succeed.

All this is human work and, therefore, subject to human error. If you're trying to diagnose an organization's performance, these are the first places to look. Managers under pressure to perform and, especially, to grow, are often tempted to pursue too many purposes at once. Failures of strategy are often failures of honesty and self-awareness—failures, in other words, to face reality. The optimism necessary to lead an organization, the essential can-do attitude of management, can easily blur into wishful thinking or worse, self-delusion. Poor strategies often rest on overestimating one's own abilities, claiming that what the organization does is a *core competence*, a source of competitive advantage, when in fact it's something that others do better. Failures of execution are often breakdowns in internal consistency, fit, and trust. The goals and metrics don't fit the purpose, they don't measure the right things. The organization says it wants x, but its system of rewards and punishments leads individuals to do y.

Second, evaluate individual managers in the context of the whole management team. Management's scope exceeds the abilities of most mere mortals. That's why it takes a team to run most organizations.

One of the reasons golf enjoys wide popularity among managers may be that it's a game where most players can't hope to make par. Like golf, management is a lot harder than it looks. In an age of increasing specialization, management may be the last refuge of the generalist. It requires both technical knowledge and human insight; it demands the perspective and the temperament to deal with enormous complexity, uncertainty, and change. It takes analysis and empathy, enthusiasm and curiosity, decisiveness and patience. Managers are skeptics who question everything, taking nothing for granted, and yet they must trust others to get the job done. If this sounds like a tall order, indeed it is. To the extent that flesh-and-blood managers disappoint us, the real problem may be that the bar is so high that few individuals ever clear it by themselves.

It's very rare for one person to excel on all dimensions. In principle, that's a simple concept to grasp. In practice, that rarely stops us from blaming individual managers for the abilities that they lack. Getting just part of it right isn't good enough. The juggler can't tell you which ball is most important. Drop just one, and the show is over. Similarly, it's not good to be inspired by someone who's leading you in the wrong direction, nor is it much better to be driven like a machine without a motivating purpose. The dual requirement of breadth and balance makes management a team sport, best played by people with complementary talents. What everyone on the team must have is integrity, and a commitment to the common mission over their own narrow self-interests.

Third, as we test management's limits in the social and public sectors, we, as citizens, will need to make decisions about the kind of value we want management to create.

As managers face new challenges, management as a discipline will continue to evolve. Unable to wait for new theory, managers will go about their business of making things work. As always, they will proceed by trial and error and, over time, new solutions will be codified and added to the existing theory and know-how we have presented. Nevertheless, the core of ideas we've discussed will endure, because it reflects both the fundamental realities of management's world and its responsibilities.

One of the great debates of the twentieth century concerned the limits of management (although people seldom thought of it in those terms). Could management be applied to organizations as large and diverse as entire economies? The answer history teaches is *no*. In the great ideological struggle between central planning and free markets, markets won hands down. At the end of the day, this mission is too diffuse, and the system too complex, to lend itself to centralized decision making.

Now we are testing management's limits in another way, by asking whether management has a role to play in fields that have traditionally been the domain of government or nonprofit organizations. Can the discipline of management, which developed largely in a commercial context, be applied to organizations in education, the arts, health care, and social services, whose purposes are very different?

As you've seen, our answer to this question is *yes*. Throughout this book, we've cited organizations that use the discipline of management to create social value in a variety of ways. Habitat for Humanity and City Year promote community and citizenship. The Nature Conservancy and the Bronx Zoo help to protect biodiversity. Aravind Eye Hospital provides health care to those unable to afford it, while Intermountain Health Care improves health care for those who can. The New York City Police Department preserves and promotes public safety.

Can the discipline make more substantial contributions to

social welfare? The answer will be *yes*, but only if we, as citizens, accept our responsibility to use it wisely. If we ask management to pursue conflicting missions—if we can't make up our minds what characterizes the educated students we want our schools to produce, or how much health care we want and at what cost—then management in those sectors will surely fall short of its potential.

But the fault will be ours and not management's. Politics is the art of compromise, enabling people with diverse interests to hang together, even though they can't agree. Management is the art of tradeoffs, taking the fork in the road best suited to the organization's purpose. Compromise may be essential in the political sphere, but it always erodes the performance of managed organizations. If an organization lacks clear objectives, by definition, its performance will suffer. In politics, there are advantages in being all things to all people. In management, that's never true.

What kind of value, then, will we ask management to create? If we want to apply management to the things we value most, we must recognize that these may also be the things that are both hardest to measure and hardest for people to agree upon. For those reasons, developing true accountability for results is the effort that must take center stage. If we want better education and health care for everyone, the essential next step will be to let management do its work of finding measures—even imperfect ones—of progress and performance. It is unlikely that a single measure—a single test score, for example—will do the job. It's a difficult mission, but not an impossible one.

Accountability may become one of the hot words of the coming decade. If so, let's hope it is because we are grappling seriously, as citizens, with an important challenge: how to measure the best things in life. These things may be priceless, but they are by no means free. Management properly applied will make them more affordable, but only if everyone takes responsibility for their part. If we ask management to do its job in arenas such as education and health care, we will have to be ready with an answer when those managers ask us what we value and what we're willing to pay for. We will have to be willing to face reality, and we will have to accept tradeoffs to accomplish our goals. That's how management works.

Sources and Related Readings

Full information is given the first time a source is cited. Subsequent citations are shortened. Additional books and articles that we think readers might find particularly interesting and/or helpful are described briefly at the end of the notes for the each chapter.

Introduction: The Universal Discipline

Peter F. Drucker's *The Practice of Management* (New York, 1954) remains the classic introduction to general management; *Managing the Nonprofit Organization: Practices and Principles* (New York, 1990) does the same for the social sector. Drucker's writing falls into two broad categories: articles, and books such as *The Effective Executive* (New York, 1966), written for managers in their capacity as managers; and works such as *Post-Capitalist Society* (Oxford, 1993) that discuss economics, politics and social issues. For anyone skeptical that a liberal imagination and an abiding interest in management can co-exist, Drucker's autobiography, *Adventures of a By-Stander* (New York, 1979) provides compelling evidence that they both can and do.

Chapter 1. Value Creation: From the Outside In

The documentary *The Wizard of Photography* is an engaging

account of George Eastman's life. It was produced by James A. DeVinney as part of the PBS series, *The American Experience*. Michael Lewis describes Silicon Graphics' failed ITV initiative in *The New, New Thing* (New York, 2000). Taylor's experiment in the science of shoveling at Bethlehem Steel is reported in *The Principles of Scientific Management* (Norcross, GA, 1998), originally published in 1911. The book is a short and interesting read for history buffs. Drucker's famous catechism appears in *The Practice of Management*. General Electric and Jack Welch are discussed in James C. Collins and Jerry I. Porras, *Built to Last: Successful Habits of Visionary Companies* (New York, 1994) and Robert Slater, *Jack Welch and the GE Way* (New York, 1999). Many of Welch's most provocative quotes are included in the compendium *Jack Welch Speaks: Wisdom from the World's Greatest Business Leader* (New York, 1998), by Janet C. Lowe. The anecdote about Martha Stewart's web site appears in Michelle Slatella's "Paying Martha Stewart a Premium for Convenience," the *New York Times*, March 2, 2000. Habitat is the subject of a Harvard Business School case by Gary Loveman and Andrew Slavitt, "Habitat for Humanity International," No. 9-694-038.

A classic exposition of the marketing mindset appears in "Marketing Myopia," Theodore Levitt's article, first published in the *Harvard Business Review* in 1975 and reprinted continuously thereafter. Vance Packard's *Hidden Persuaders* (New York, 1957) is one of the early explorations of the psychology of advertising. An instructive and engaging introduction to the merger and takeover mania of the 1980s is *Barbarians at the Gates: The Fall of RJR Nabisco* (New York, 1990) by Bryan Burroughs and John Helyar, who covered many of the decade's more notorious deals for the *Wall Street Journal*. If the phrase *supply-chain management* makes your eyes glaze over, see Joan Magretta's interview with Victor Fung, "Fast, Global and Entrepreneurial: Supply Chain

Management, Hong Kong Style," in *Harvard Business Review,* 1998, subsequently included in her collection, *Managing in the New Economy* (Boston, 1999).

Chapter 2. Business Models: Converting Insight to Enterprise

"Discovery-Driven Planning" by Rita McGrath and Ian MacMillan (*Harvard Business Review,* 1995) uses the EuroDisney story and others to connect the narrative logic of a business model and the numbers that must add up. American Express is one of the companies Collins and Porras examine in *Built to Last.* Fargo's story is told in Daniel Gross's highly readable collection, *Forbes Greatest Business Stories of All Time* (New York, 1996). Michael Bronner's college enterprise is described in the Harvard Business School case "Bronner Slosberg Humphrey," No. 9-598-136, by David E. Bell and Donald M. Leavitt. Since the late 1990s, eBay has been the subject of enormous press attention. The material used here is drawn from another Harvard Business School case, Nicole Tempest, "Meg Whitman at eBay, Inc. (A)," No. 9-400-035. Many of the insights into Dell's business model come from Joan Magretta's interview with Michael Dell, "The Power of Virtual Integration," published in *Harvard Business Review* in 1998 and reprinted in *Managing in the New Economy.* Bratton's transformation of New York City's Police Department is the subject of James L. Heskett's Harvard Business School case, "NYPD New," No. 9-396-293. The founding of Elderhostel is described by Eugene S. Mill in *The Story of Elderhostel* (Hanover, N.H., 1993). The decisions City Year's management faced as they thought about expanding the program beyond Boston are part of the Harvard Business School case, "City Year: National Expansion Strategy (A)," No. 9-496-001 by Nicole Sackley.

Alfred D. Chandler, Jr., *The Visible Hand: The Managerial Revolution in American Business* (Cambridge, MA, 1977) was the first (and is still the classic) account of the role of management in the development of large-scale industrial enterprises. As a company, 3M is famous for telling stories. In "Strategic Stories: How 3M is Rewriting Business Planning," *Harvard Business Review*, 1998, Gordon Shaw, a 3M executive, and two co-authors explain why (and how) narratives can be a far more effective way of communicating a company's business plan than bullet-point lists. Robert Heilbroner and Lester Thurow, *Economics Explained* (New York, 1994) is a wonderful introduction to, or refresher course in, the dismal science, which includes a very good section on how markets work and where they fail. *Information Rules*, by Carl Shapiro and Hal Varian (Boston, 1998) provides a sensible explanation of how the old rules of microeconomics apply in an economy increasingly driven by bits and bytes.

Chapter 3. Strategy: The Logic of Superior Performance

The fundamental premise of this chapter, that strategy is about doing better by being different, is laid out in Michael Porter's article, "What Is Strategy?" *Harvard Business Review*, 1996. The business information about Wal*Mart that appears throughout this chapter can be found in Sharon Foley (revised by Takia Mahmood), "Wal*Mart Stores, Inc.," Harvard Business School Case, No. 9-794-024. Walton gives his own account of his company and his life in *Sam Walton, Made in America*, with John Huey (New York, 1992). To understand Japan's economic problems in the 1990s, see Michael Porter, Hirotaka Takeuchi, and Mariko Sakakibara, *Can Japan Compete?* (New York, 2000). The quip about lumberjacks and generals comes from Avinash Dixit and Barry J. Nalebuff, *Thinking Strategically* (New York, 1991). Theirs is a smart and witty book that captures the dynamic, interactive dimension of strategy as it plays out in business and in everyday life. Adam Brandenburger and Barry Nalebuff lay out the basics of game theory as applied to business strategy in "The Right Game: Use Game Theory to Shape Strategy," *Harvard Business*

Review, 1995. The original and still the best presentation of the five forces is in Michael E. Porter's classic "How Competitive Forces Shape Strategy," *Harvard Business Review*, 1979. David Lawrence's argument about mission and performance is made in "Maintaining a Mission: Lessons from the Marketplace," *Leader to Leader*, 1999. The quotes from John Sawhill are taken from "Surviving Success," an interview with Alice Howard and Joan Magretta published in *Harvard Business Review*, 1995.

For anyone who wants to understand the microeconomic framework that underpins strategy, Michael Porter's *Competitive Advantage* (New York, 1985) is *the* place to start. Porter's articles are collected in *On Competition* (Boston, 1998), which provides a sweeping overview of his work, not only on competitive strategy, but also corporate strategy and national competitiveness. To get a front-row view of strategy in action, and how industries change, there may be no better book than Andy Grove's *Only the Paranoid Survive: How to Exploit the Crisis Points that Challenge Every Company and Career* (New York, 1996). The strategy discussed throughout this chapter is competitive strategy—the strategy of a single business. Corporate strategy, the strategy for an organization made up of many businesses (such as GE) is another kettle of fish. A good introduction and starting point is the 1998 *Harvard Business Review* article, "Creating Corporate Advantage," by David Collis and Cynthia Montgomery.

Chapter 4. Organization: Where to Draw the Lines
Short accounts of the Ford story can be found in Gross, *Forbes Greatest Business Stories* and in Collins and Porras, *Built to Last*. One of the most engaging histories of the U.S. auto industry and its fateful encounter with Japanese rivals is David Halberstam, *The Reckoning* (New York, 1986). The standard biography of Henry Ford is Allan Nevins, *Ford: The Times, the Man, the Company* (New

York, 1954). Chandler, *The Visible Hand,* uses General Motors to illustrate the rise of the multidivisional company. For a personal account of the company's evolution, see Alfred P. Sloan, Jr.'s, *My Years With General Motors* (Garden City, 1964). Cisco's extraordinary rise is the subject of David Bunnell, *Making the Cisco Connection: The Story Behind the Real Internet Superpower* (New York, 2000). Aravind Eye Hospital is the subject of Kasturi Rangan, "The Aravind Eye Hospital, Madurai, India: In Service for Sight," Harvard Business School Case, No. 9-593-098 and Harriet Rubin, "The Perfect Vision of Dr. V," *Fast Company,* 2001.

For readers who want to delve deeply into the theory of organization, we recommend Paul R. Milgrom and John Roberts, *Economics, Organization and Management* (Englewood Cliffs, NJ, 1992). Yes, it's a text, and it weighs fifteen pounds, but it ties together many of the topics discussed in Part I clearly and comprehensively. An excellent study of the lean manufacturing system pioneered by Toyota is James P. Womack, Daniel T. Jones, and Daniel Roos, *The Machine That Changed the World* (Cambridge, MA, 1990).

Chapter 5. Facing Reality: Which Numbers Matter and Why

The data on six sigma comes from Slater, *Jack Welch and the GE Way.* The story of Robert McNamara, the Whiz Kids, and the Ford Pinto debacle is told in Andrea Gabor, *The Capitalist Philosophers: The Geniuses of Modern Business—Their Lives, Times, and Ideas* (New York, 2000). Her book is a well-written history of management ideas, as well as the human beings who developed and articulated them. The quote from John Allen Paulos can be found in *Once Upon a Number: The Hidden Mathematical Logic of Stories* (New York, 1998).

For readers who feel insecure about dealing with data, David Maister, "How to Avoid Getting Lost in the Numbers," Harvard

Business School Case, No. 9-682-010 provides a helpful antidote. See also Robert Dolan, "Note on Low-Tech Marketing Math," Harvard Business School Case, No. 9-599-011 for the basics on fixed and variable costs, and the math of margins. John Allen Paulos, *Innumeracy: Mathematical Illiteracy and Its Consequences* (New York, 1988) argues persuasively and engagingly that in modern society, citizens must be as comfortable interpreting information presented numerically as they are with information presented in words.

Chapter 6. The *Real* Bottom Line: Mission and Measures
Information about the Hershey School's dilemma comes from an article by Daniel Goldin, "Mr. Hershey's Wishes," in the *Wall Street Journal*, August 12, 1999. Ford's unconventional practices are described in Collins and Porras, *Built to Last*. Sloan describes GM's measurement—and management—challenge in *My Years With General Motors*. Greg Brenneman's first person account of the Continental turnaround, "Right Away and All At Once: How We Saved Continental" was published in *Harvard Business Review*, 1998. The quotes from Fidelity's Ellyn McColgan are taken from an unpublished interview with Joan Magretta. Dell's metrics are described in "The Power of Virtual Integration"; Bratton's in "NYPD New." John Sawhill explains the revision of The Nature Conservancy's measures in "Surviving Success."

Read together, the stories recounted in *Built to Last* provide powerful evidence of the performance that can be created when a company's management reflects its purpose with the right measures.

Chapter 7. Betting on the Future: Innovation and Uncertainty
Sloan's marketing insights are from *My Years With General Motors*. For Andy Grove's comments see *Only the Paranoid Survive*. The anecdotes about 3M and Hewlett-Packard come from Collins and

Porras, *Built to Last*. Drucker has been teaching managers that their work includes entrepreneurship for almost half a century, most recently in *Management Challenges for the 21ˢᵗ Century* (New York, 1999). The material about Schwab throughout this chapter is from David S. Pottruck and Terry Pearce, *Clicks and Mortar: Passion-Driven Growth in an Internet-Driven World* (San Francisco, 2000). "The Innovator's Lament" appeared on a note handed to Peter Bernstein at a conference. He tells the story in *Against the Gods: The Remarkable Story of Risk* (New York, 1996). The Xerox story is part of the saga recounted in Douglas K. Smith and Robert C. Alexander, *Fumbling the Future: How Xerox Invented, Then Ignored, the First Personal Computer* (New York, 1988). An account of Scolnick's gamble appears in Gardner Harris, "With Big Drugs Dying, Merck Didn't Merge—It Found New Ones," the *Wall Street Journal*, January 10, 2001.

With finance, as with organization, the best way to understand the basics is with a clear, well-written text. In finance, the classic (now in its sixth edition) is Richard A. Brearley and Stewart C. Myers, *Principles of Corporate Finance* (Boston, 2000). To understand the challenges that new technologies pose to established companies, see Clayton M. Christensen, *The Innovator's Dilemma: When New Technologies Cause Great Firms to Fail* (Boston, 1997). A readable and very practical guide to using decision analysis at work and in your private life is *Smart Choices: A Practical Guide to Making Better Decisions* (Boston, 1999) by John S. Hammond, Ralph L. Keeney, and Howard Raiffa.

Chapter 8. Delivering Results: First, You Focus

Welch's bottom line on the CEO's job appears in Slater, *Jack Welch and the GE Way*. Walton explains his view of continuous improvement and, later, its application to Wal*Mart's operations in Walton, *Sam Walton: Made In American*. eBay's use of the 80-20 rule is described in Tempest, "Meg Whitman at eBay." Humana's story is part of a Public Broadcasting System documentary, *Critical Condition: Inside American Medicine*, produced by Hedrick Smith. Cindy Williams, a research scientist at MIT, describes the Defense Department's budgeting practices in "Redeploy the Dollars," the *New York Times*, February 16, 2001. Jack Greenberg is quoted in Jennifer Ordonez, "An Efficiency Drive: Fast-Food Lanes Are Getting Even Faster," the *Wall Street Journal*, May 18, 2000. Information on the best-practice initiatives at Intermountain Health and the Northern New England Collaborative comes from "Critical Condition." Minnesota's health-care initiative is reported in Milt Freudenhein's "Minnesota Health Plans to Standardize Treatments," the *New York Times*, March 13, 2001.

Hammond, et. al., *Smart Choices*, provides an excellent introduction to the psychology of decision making.

Chapter 9. Managing People: Which Values Matter and Why

Welch's typology of managers is reported in Lowe, *Jack Welch Speaks*. Charles A. O'Reilly III and Jeffrey Pfeffer write about Southwest in *Hidden Value: How Great Companies Achieve Extraordinary Results with Ordinary People* (Boston, 2000). Information about Southwest's culture here and throughout the chapter comes from their book. Scott McNealy is quoted in "it's like . . . businesses built on metaphors still need value," *Forbes ASAP*, October 2, 2000. The Verizon story was reported by Mary Williams Walsh, "When 'May I Help You' Is a Labor Issue," the *New York Times*, August 12, 2000. Colleen Barrett's comment about watching new hires closely appears in Matthew Brelis, "Herb's Way," the *Boston Globe*, November 5, 2000. Michael Lewis's account of Silicon Graphics's misadventures with psychological testing in *The New New Thing* is both funny and appalling. Taylor's advice on performance feedback comes from *Principles of Scientific Management*.

Marvin Buckingham and Curt Coffman capture the important elements of managing people in *First Break All the Rules: What the World's Greatest Managers Do Differently* (New York, 1999). As you'll discover if you read the book, however, what makes great managers great isn't that they break the rules but, rather, that they actually practice them. For a lucid lesson in what real participatory management involves see W. Chan Kim and Renee Mauborgne, "Fair Process: Managing in the Knowledge Economy," *Harvard Business Review*, 1997. Peter Drucker's advice on "Managing Oneself" is included in *Management Challenges for the 21st Century*. A classic, highly practical introduction to negotiation is Roger Fisher and William Ury, with Bruce Patton, ed., *Getting to Yes: Negotiating Agreement Without Giving In* (Boston, 1981).

Index